A Lifetime Worth Remembering
~ *From Orphan to Hero*

JOHN W. BRAUCHT

His life as told to Barbara Cronin Harrington

JWB Publishing
St. Petersburg, Florida

first published in 2000 by
JWB Publishing
St. Petersburg, Florida

Copyright © 2000 by John W. Braucht
Cover Illustration copyright © 2000 by Linda L. Russ
Interior Text Design copyright © 2000 by Jan Dunn

The sale of this book without its cover is unauthorized. If you purchase this book without a cover, you should be aware that it was reported to the publisher as "unsold or destroyed". Neither the author nor the publisher has received payment for the sale of this "stripped book".

All rights reserved. No part of this book may be reproduced or transmitted in any form or by any means, electronic or mechanical, including photocopy, recording or by any information storage and retrieval system, without the written permission of the Publisher, except where permitted by law.

Library of Congress #: LCCN 00-092508   ISBN #: 0-9703491-9-X

ACKNOWLEDGEMENTS

To my precious wife, Luella, who made this book possible with her love and devotion; and my sons, Gene and Ricky, with my beautiful granddaughters, Ginger and Jodie and grandsons, Robert and Shane and five great grandchildren.

Also, to those who are no longer with us: my brother, Owen Lay, my mother and father, Marie and Glen, Known as "G.B", and the grandest man I have ever known, grandfather John Clarke.

I would also like to acknowledge people in my life who have influenced and helped me in so many ways: Reverend Cloninger, Dr. W. H. Sims, Dr. John Caylor, Reverend Orville Griffin, R. Clay Kent, Rick Farwell, Earl Brown, Marvin Rice, Jim and Sue Coram, Morris Hann, Tom Harter, Dr. Basil Jackson, Mike Fitzpatrick, Vance Van Hall, Max Benny, Ken Pridemore, Willard Rogers, Willard Breckenridge and Jack Ayers.

To all those I knew and served with during the twenty-four years of military service in the Infantry, Coast Artillery AA and the various organizations branches and fields in the United States Air Force.

And a special thanks to Linda L. Russ, the talented artist who illustrated and designed the cover for this book.

There are so many more that to tell about them would take another book

John W. Braucht

FOREWORD

I was delighted and honored when my good friend, John Braucht, asked me to write a foreword for this book. I am delighted to do so. The only problem I had in fulfilling this request was that my wife got hold of the manuscript and became so interested in John's story that I had a difficult time retrieving it.

The book is just as fascinating as John. It is an account which is full of pathos, pain, sorrow, excitement, enthusiasm and joy. It is a story replete with Americana and an insider's experience of everything from abandonment and The Great Depression to military adventures, including being shot down over the English Channel.

Above everything else, however, it is the story of a good man, full of faith and determination to serve his God and to teach others what he has been privileged to learn, both in the world and in the Word.

This all adds up to an evocative and wonderful story, which I have thoroughly enjoyed.

Basil Jackson, M.D.

PROLOGUE

I was about five years old when my parents dropped me and my two younger brothers, Clyde and Owen off at a stranger's house in San Antonio, Texas. It was the last time we ever saw them.

A LIFETIME WORTH REMEMBERING

"HERBERT McLEAN EVANS AND K.J. SCOTT DISCOVER VITAMIN E"

Chapter One
1922

I remember my Papa shaking me by the shoulders. "Wake up, Homer," he said. "We're going for a long ride."

It was early in the morning and I was half-asleep, but I remember climbing into the back seat of his big open black car with my little brothers. Papa drove for a long time and when it grew dark, he pulled alongside a field and parked.

"I'm too tired to drive any more tonight," he told Mama. "You sleep in the back seat. I need to stretch out my legs."

She climbed in the back with my brothers and me, but it was too crowded and my brothers started whining.

"You'll have to sleep on the running board, Homer," Papa said. "There's not enough room back there for everyone."

It was so dark outside that I could only see the stars in the sky. "I don't want to, Papa," I said. "I'm scared of the dark."

"Don't be a baby, Homer. There's nothing to be afraid of. Now hurry. I need to get some rest."

JOHN BRAUCHT

I had no choice but to do as my Papa said. Reluctantly, I got out of the car and curled up on the running board. It was hard and uncomfortable and I couldn't sleep. Before long, my imagination began to run away with me. I remembered pictures of elephants and hippopotamus that I had seen in a book and imagined those huge beasts thundering out of the nearby field to eat me up. I was too frightened to stay outside so I crawled in the back of the car as quietly as possible and squeezed in at Mama's feet where I felt safe, and fell sound asleep.

As soon as it was daylight, Papa started driving again and before long, pulled up in front of a big house. He jumped out of the car, reached in the back seat and scooped Clyde and Owen up in his arms.

"It would be easier for everyone if you stayed in the car," he said to Mama. "I'll take the boys inside."

I remember that Mama had tears in her eyes as she bent over to kiss us. "Promise you'll take good care of Clyde and Owen," she cried, hugging me so tight I could hardly breathe.

"I promise Mama," I said.

"And no matter what, Homer, always remember Papa and I love you very much. Okay?"

"Okay," I agreed. I didn't understand what was going on and sensed something was very wrong. Papa started toward the house and motioned me to follow. I got out of the car, and waved goodbye to Mama, then hurried to catch up to Papa. I grabbed hold of his sleeve as he climbed the steps to the front porch.

A woman who I had never seen before opened the

A LIFETIME WORTH REMEMBERING

door and smiled.

"Come in," she said. "We've been expecting you."

As we stepped into the entryway, Papa placed Clyde in her arms and lowered Owen to the floor. He whispered something in the woman's ear then knelt down in front of me.

"You're a big boy now, Homer," he said. "You're almost five years old and you have to be brave and watch over Owen and Clyde." He pointed to the woman. "This is Mrs. Anderson. She's going to take care of you for a while."

"I don't want to stay here!" I screamed. "I want to go home with you and Mama!"

Papa stood up and brushed the tears away with his sleeve.

"We have no choice, do you understand? We have to leave you here."

My lip trembled and I started to cry. "Yes, Papa," I said, but I did not understand. All I understood was that I was frightened.

He kissed us goodbye, turned abruptly and walked toward the door. "We'll be back at Christmas," he said over his shoulder, never once looking back.

Owen started bawling and I put my arm around him. "Don't cry, Papa will be back soon." Clyde, who was too young to realize what was going on, stood next to me and clutched my hand.

We stayed with Mrs. Anderson for what seemed like a long time. I missed my parents, and was looking forward to Christmas, the day Papa said he would be back for us.

JOHN BRAUCHT

We never had enough to eat. Sometimes I stole food from the icebox on the back porch for my brothers and me. Mrs. Anderson used to leave us alone a lot and I was scared. Before long, some people came to the house.

"We're taking you and your brothers to the orphanage," a man said.

"What about my Papa?" I asked, afraid that he wouldn't know where we were. "How will he find us?"

"Don't worry, Mrs. Anderson will let him know where you are," the man assured me.

I would later learn that someone reported Mrs. Anderson to the child abuse authorities for leaving us alone at night. And it would be years later when I discovered that my brothers and I had been abandoned by our parents and taken into custody by the state.

The people who took us to the orphanage gave us candy and were kind to us.

"We're going to take you to a real nice place," the woman said while we were driving.

"You'll have lots of toys and friends to play with."

As we drove up a long driveway, the man pointed to a big wooden building with a screened-in porch. "That's the orphanage, Homer."

That big building and the yard, overrun with laughing children is still vivid in my mind. They were playing on swings and seesaws and for a moment I forgot my fear. I wanted to run and join them, but Owen looked frightened and hugged my arm. I took his hand and we followed the man and woman inside to a big office.

"You're going to stay here with us for a while," Mrs.

A LIFETIME WORTH REMEMBERING

Bliss, the administrator of the orphanage, said as she stood up from behind her desk. "You'll like it here, Homer. You're going to have lots of friends to play with."

I shrugged. I had no other choice.

A friendly looking woman entered the room and smiled at me. "This is Maggie," Mrs. Bliss said. "She's one of the matrons here and she's going to take your brothers with her now and get them settled in their rooms."

Maggie looked at me, as if to say it would be all right. She took Clyde with one hand, Owen by the other and started to leave the room, when Owen wrenched free and ran back to me. Maggie grabbed his arm but he struggled to get away.

"No, it's okay, darlin'" she said. "I'm just going to take you to your room."

"I want Homer!" he screamed. "I want to stay with my brother!"

I tried to go to him, but was held back by the man. "No, Homer, you can't go with him. You have your own room with boys your age. Your brothers are too young to stay with you but you'll get to see them later."

I watched Clyde and Owen being carried off, sobbing and screaming for me. I bit my lip to keep from crying and yelled out, "Don't worry!"

Maggie returned after a few minutes, and took me to a large room filled with small wrought-iron bunk beds.

"This is the dormitory," she said, walking over to a corner bed. "This is where you'll sleep." She pointed to the upper bunk. "Up there, in the top. And these two lockers are yours. They're for your clothes and toys."

"I don't have any clothes or toys," I said. "I don't

have anything."

She gave me a hug. "Well, don't worry honey. You're going to get lots of things."

She stayed with me until it was suppertime, then took me down into the dining room. Everywhere I looked, boys and girls were seated at long tables. Finally I spotted Clyde sitting at a table across the room. I looked at Maggie.

"Go sit with your brother, Homer. You'll both feel better," Maggie said.

Clyde stopped crying the moment he saw me then crawled on my lap, stuck his thumb in his mouth and fell asleep. I sat there, fascinated, and watched the children wolf down their meals, surprised to see some snatching food out of the other's plates.

It wasn't long after we were settled at the orphanage, that Mrs. Bliss called me to her office. I thought that maybe my parents had come for us.

"I have something to tell you, Homer."

"Is my Mama and Papa here?" I asked.

She looked sad. "No, not yet," she said, her expression changing to a smile. "But I do have some good news. Your little brother Clyde has been adopted and—"

"What does that mean," I interrupted.

"It means he's going to live with a nice family?" she explained.

"Why?" I asked.

"Well, Homer. When he first came here, he was pretty sick. He had what they call malnutrition."

I was puzzled. "Mal, maltrunition? What's that?"

A LIFETIME WORTH REMEMBERING

She smiled as I struggled to pronounce the word. "Clyde didn't get the right kind of food before he came here and he almost went to heaven. They said that the doctor who examined him didn't expect him to live. But the doctor's taking good care of him and he's going to be fine now."

"I want to see Clyde."

"I'm afraid you can't Homer. He's with his new mama and papa."

"But he has a mama and papa," I said. "He doesn't need new ones."

Mrs. Bliss shook her head. "Don't you want your brother to be happy and healthy?"

I thought about what she said and responded, "I guess I do." The word 'adopted' didn't really mean much at the time. All I knew was that I missed my baby brother and wanted to see him.

They put up a big Christmas tree in the dining room. The kids were excited at the thoughts of Santa Claus and the toys he would bring.

All I wanted was my parents to come back like my father promised. "Is it Christmas yet?" I asked everyday. And they kept saying, "Not yet."

Finally they said, "Yes, tomorrow is Christmas, and tonight Santa Claus is coming down the chimney."

I was happy that Santa Claus was coming, but it was more important that my parents were coming. I sat waiting for them by the front door for hours.

"It's time for bed, Homer," Maggie said.

"Where's my papa and momma, Maggie? They said

they'd come and get us at Christmas."

"Don't you worry," Maggie said, trying to cheer me up. "You and Owen are going to a big party at Mrs. Lay's house tomorrow. She's a nice lady and you'll have fun there."

I tried not to think about my parents that night, and thought of the party instead.

We no sooner arrived at Mrs. Lay's party, than she picked up Owen.

"Oh my goodness!" she cried. "This is horrible! Just look at this poor child's head. It's covered with sores!"

Her husband took a closer look. "It looks like a bad case of cradle cap. This poor child needs a lot of care."

Mr. and Mrs. Lay were very kind and made sure all the kids enjoyed the party. She especially made a fuss over Owen and me the entire night.

It was only a few days later, when Mr. and Mrs. Lay came to the orphanage and I was called in to the office. Mrs. Lay knelt down in front of me.

"We want to adopt your little brother, Homer," she said. "My husband and I would love to have a little boy, and we'll take really good care of him."

I didn't know what to say. I still did not understand what adoption meant. All I knew was that they were going to take Owen away from me just as the doctor had taken Clyde. I found my voice and said, "But I don't want you to take him."

"You want him to be happy, don't you?"

"Yes Ma'am," I said.

"And you want his head to get better, don't you?"

"Yes," I repeated, remembering how sickly Owen had been.

"Then, my husband and I are going to see that he has the

A LIFETIME WORTH REMEMBERING

best care and we'll love him just like he's our own little boy. Do you understand now?"

"I think so," I said.

That night, I said a prayer for my brothers and cried my self to sleep.

A few days later, Mrs. Bliss called me into her office again. Mrs. Lay had returned and was smiling at me. I looked around for my brother. "Where's Owen?" I asked.

"He's home with my husband," Mrs. Lay answered. "You remember how sick he was. Well, the doctor didn't think he'd live through the night, but we took such good care of him that he's all better now."

I was happy that Owen wasn't sick anymore but I missed him very much. "Can I see him?"

"Well, that's why I'm here. How would you like us to adopt you too."

I thought about it for a few moments, but by that time, I was adjusted to the orphanage and was happy with my new found friends "Are there lots of kids to play with at your house?" I asked.

"No, darling, just Owen."

Again I mulled it over in my mind. "No. No thank you, Ma'am. I think I'd like to stay here and play with my friends."

JOHN BRAUCHT

"THE DISCOVERY OF INSULIN WINS SIR FREDERICK BANTING OF CANADA AND JOHN J.R. McCLEOD OF ENGLAND THE NOBEL PRIZE"

Chapter Two
1923

The remainder of my stay at the orphanage for the most part was a pleasant one, as I recall. The children were not mistreated. There was always enough food to eat, and toys to play with and I was never without a friend.

On Saturday mornings we were taken to the picture shows as they were called then. I remember how scared I used to be watching those adventure movies on the big screen. Thunderous sounds blasted from the orchestra pit to add life to the silence of the films. One particular movie, "The Ten Commandments" had me so frightened that I ran out to the lobby and hid until the show was over.

At Easter I went on my first egg hunt and later, when the weather turned warmer, I went swimming at the Breckenridge Park pool. Once I strayed into the deep end and thought I was going to drown. I screamed for help and

JOHN BRAUCHT

a beautiful lady in a blue dress jumped in and pulled me to safety. That kind lady will always remain in my mind.

One time, someone stole some money from the office. When no one owned up to the theft, all the kids were punished. The matrons made us bend over the short locker, and paddled our rear ends. Other times, if we misbehaved, we were given a strong dose of castor oil. When it got to be my turn, I gagged on its thick oily taste, but they made sure that I swallowed enough to suffer its effects. Then I'd throw up, and they'd make me clean up the mess. I can still taste that horrible stuff in my mouth to this day.

Saturday night was bath time. A big tub was filled with hot water and by the time it was my turn to climb in, the water was dirty and cold. Maybe five to ten kids had to use the same water, sometimes two at a time if they were small enough.

We slept on the floor at naptime so we wouldn't mess up the beds. One time a boy was stung by a scorpion and from that day on, I refused to sleep on the floor.

I wasn't at the orphanage long before we were relocated to a larger building on a big farm with lots of animals. I had never seen a goat or a pig before. I never even had a pet.

My only experience to the outside world was the Easter hunt and trips to Breckenridge Park. Other than that, we were completely isolated from the rest of the world.

I loved being on the farm. The cows, horses, chickens and pigs that were off limits to the kids were a constant source of temptation. The older kids were expected to work the crops. I was either too young or too small and wasn't given any responsibilities.

A LIFETIME WORTH REMEMBERING

Some of my friends discovered a small creek about a half-mile away. During the rainy season we went swimming there in our underwear but when it was dry and the creek started to dry out...we discovered catfish floundering in the shallow puddles of water. We caught them with our bare hands, which left our hands bleeding from their thorny barbs.

Eventually I was put to work gathering rocks for the garden. It was hot out in the sun and the older boys constructed a crude framework shelter. Some of the smaller kids gathering palm fronds for the roof found some gunnysacks behind an old shed. We nailed boards between two limbs and strung the sacks under the boards, making a sort of hammock. I felt tired and wanted to test the hammock out, so I climbed in it.

An older boy named Joey ran over to me. "Hey, you!" he yelled. "You get out of there!"

"It's not your tree!" I said, refusing to budge. I probably should have listened to him, because the next thing I knew, he whacked me on the head with a rock and it was sore for a week.

The women who worked in the kitchen were kind. When we were hungry between meals, they gave us snacks like bread pudding and pecans. Sometimes they gave us crackers with weevils in them, but after we gave them a few good shakes, the bugs fell out. We didn't let a few weevils stop us from enjoying the crackers. But the bread pudding was the best. It was cut into solid squares, just perfect enough to hold in your hand without making a mess. It was delicious and to this day, I haven't tasted any bread pudding as good.

The only time anyone got to eat ice cream is when you

were sick. Sometimes I wished I were sick just so that I could have some ice cream. The wish never came true as long as I was in the orphanage, but after I left, I ate more than my share.

We were given a few pecans from time to time, and my friend Aubrey found a way to play a game with them.

"You give me your pecan," Aubrey asked a younger boy. "I bet I can crack your nut with my fist and if I can't you get to keep both of them."

The younger boy handed his pecan to Aubrey. "Okay. I'll play."

Aubrey placed the pecan side by side with his pecan, and made a fist. When he opened his hand, the boy's nut was smashed. "I get to keep it!" Aubrey yelled triumphantly.

"Now it's my turn to try," another boy said, handing his pecan to Aubrey. Aubrey cracked the second nut as easily as he had the first.

Some of the kids tried to crack other kids pecans and were successful. But when it was Aubrey's turn, he always won. Aubrey was the best at the game and after a while no one wanted to play the game with him.

Aubrey usually gave me back my pecan when the other kids weren't around. One day, he pulled me aside.

"Can you keep a secret, Homer?" he asked.

"Sure," I answered.

"Cross your heart and swear you'll never tell," he insisted.

I made a cross over my heart and promised. "Cross my heart and hope to die, I will never tell."

Aubrey looked around and making sure that no one could see him, he reached into his pocket and withdrew a

A LIFETIME WORTH REMEMBERING

small rock. At first glance it looked exactly like a pecan. A big grin spread across his face.

"This is my lucky charm. No one can crack this beauty."

"But that's cheating," I said.

He shook his head. "Naw, it's not. It's part of the game. And I was the smartest."

I suppose I had to agree, but I still didn't think it was fair to the other kids.

Sometimes we played a game where someone would close their eyes and be carried off someplace and put on the ground. Then they had to guess where they were. If they guessed correctly, it was their turn to carry the next kid away. When it was my turn to be carried off, it didn't take long to guess where I was. They had placed me on a bed of large red ants. Another experience I cannot forget.

There was always a pile of used lumber left behind the shed. Using our imagination, we built a clubhouse with a tunnel that was barely wide or high enough for us to crawl through. The old lumber had rusty nails sticking out. Since there was nothing to remove them with but rocks, we'd hammer them flat as best we could, which sometimes wasn't good enough. Whenever we crawled through the tunnel, the nails tore at our clothes and ripped at our skin but we didn't mind...we were having fun.

One time, we had a contest to see who could make the biggest ball out of string. I got lucky and found an old sweater that I unraveled. I wound the yarn into the biggest ball and was declared the winner.

JOHN BRAUCHT

"WILLEN EINTHOVEN OF THE NETHERLANDS WINS THE NOBEL PRIZE FOR INVENTING THE ELECTROCARDIOGRAPH"

Chapter Three
1924

I must have been around seven when they said it was time for me to start school. Some older boys were supposed to take me on the first day. We were walking through a path of cactus plants and thick bushes, when one of the boys stopped and looked me straight in the eyes and said, "We don't go to school, Homer, so you don't have to go either."

"But I'm supposed to go," I protested.

The biggest boy grabbed me by the shirt. "So what! We don't care."

"But I'll get in trouble if someone finds out," I said weakly.

"Nobody's gonna find out, and you better never tell anyone," he threatened, tightening the shirt around my neck. "You understand?"

"I understand," I mumbled. All I understood was that he was going to hurt me if I told on them. He didn't have to persuade me further, because I really didn't want to go to school anyway. For several hours we sat around in a field telling stories and eating cactus fruit. Eating the fruit was an education in itself. First you had to learn how to touch the prickly red berries without the stickers shooting into your hands. It took quite a bit of practice and many tries before I succeeded getting the berries into my mouth. But eating them was another ballgame. It took a lot of times before I was actually able to eat one and I spent the rest of the day picking the stickers out of my hands and lips. By that time my fingers and lips were dyed bright red.

Sometimes we'd spend the day hanging around some of the older townspeople who enjoyed telling us stories of their youthful experiences. One old-timer took the time to show us how to whittle little animals and dolls.

I don't know why no one ever discovered that I wasn't going to school. I guess back in the twenties, things were different. There weren't any truant officers, and it didn't seem to matter to the people at the orphanage if we got an education or not. Their priority was to get us adopted.

Looking back, I'm sure adopting older children proved to be difficult, if not impossible, especially when times were not prosperous.

All the kids looked forward to Christmas. People felt sorry for us and donated clothes and toys to the orphanage. One year I received a pair of tan trousers, which were my first grown up pants. They were the nicest present I ever got so I folded them carefully and placed them in my locker. When I looked for them the next day, they were gone.

A LIFETIME WORTH REMEMBERING

Maggie searched all the lockers and asked the boys if they had taken the pants, but no one ever owned up to the theft and the pants were never found. Maggie knew that I was very disappointed, and she saw to it that I was given a new pair.

It was after several of my friends went to live with families when my best friend Aubrey was adopted. Until then, I didn't mind living at the orphanage. But when Aubrey left, I was pretty lonely. By now I fully understood what the word adoption meant, and I liked the sound of it.

"I want a mother and father like the other kids," I said to Maggie one day. "Why haven't I been adopted?"

She smiled at me. "You didn't seem to care before, Homer. You always seem happy and content so we passed you by. Besides, remember you had a chance to be adopted with your little brother."

I nodded, wishing that I had gone with him. "But I want to be adopted now," I said.

"Then I'll speak to Mrs. Bliss and see what we can do. I'm sure we can find someone who wants a good little boy like you."

A few weeks later, Mrs. Bliss gave me the good news…I was going to be adopted by a nice family who owned a grocery store in town. Mr. and Mrs. Davis, a middle-aged couple, agreed to take me on a trial basis.

"We're glad you're with us, Homer and we hope everything will work out so you can become our son. But you have to behave yourself. We don't want a disobedient boy. Now, would you like to see the store?"

JOHN BRAUCHT

"Yes, Ma'am," I said eagerly.

Mrs. Davis walked ahead of me, explaining everything about the store. "Now, Homer, we don't want you to touch anything here without our permission," she said, turning to face me. "Especially those weights." She pointed to a set of scales. "We use them to weigh the meat and if you drop one of them on the glass, it would cost a lot of money to replace." She walked over to a large brown crock on the counter. "This is the cookie jar but remember, you are not to touch it without our permission."

"I promise, Ma'am," I said, even though I knew it would be a huge temptation not to. "I won't touch anything." My mouth was already watering for the contents of that cookie jar and my hands itched to touch all the wonderful things that I had never seen before.

I spent several days following her around, learning where things belonged. "There is a time for everything, Homer," Mrs. Davis would say, "and a place for everything."

After I was there awhile, I was allowed to sweep the floor and dust the cans and jars on the shelves. I didn't mind. Sometimes I even got to wait on customers. I began to learn my numbers by reading the price tags that were marked on the goods. I enjoyed working there and felt proud when Mrs. Davis introduced me to the customers and friends as her new son.

And the best part was that I got to eat all the stale and broken cookies.

Everything was going great. Now I had parents like the other kids.

But my happiness was short lived.

A LIFETIME WORTH REMEMBERING

Business was slow one day, when Mr. Davis said, "We have to do an errand, Homer. Don't touch anything. We'll be back in about ten minutes."

It was the first time I was alone in the store and the temptation to play with the forbidden weights made me forget my promise. I was nervous and my hands were sweating when I picked up the biggest weight, but it was so heavy that it slipped out of my hands and shattered the glass counter top.

Mr. and Mrs. Davis returned just in time to hear the crash. Needless to say, they were very upset.

Mr. Davis shook his head. "We can't trust you anymore, Homer. We have no choice but to send you back."

I felt really sorry, but sorry was too late.

And that was the end of adoption number one.

But my unhappiness didn't last long. The next day, Mr. Jenkins, a kind old man, drove me back to the orphanage in his covered wagon, pulled by a pinto pony.

"What happened? Why are they sending you back?" he asked.

"I broke my promise and touched something I wasn't supposed to touch," I confessed.

"I suppose you learned a hard lesson."

"A very hard lesson, Sir."

"Don't worry, Homer. You're a fine young man." He patted me on the back, "And some couple is going to be lucky to adopt you as their son."

His words of comfort made me feel better.

A few weeks later, I thought his words were going to come true when Mrs. Bliss called me into her office.

"Well, Homer, you have a second chance to be adopted. And this time you better be a good boy and don't do anything wrong. Do you understand?"

"Yes, Ma'am," I said without hesitation. "I definitely understand."

Mr. and Mrs. Birch, a gentleman farmer and his wife, lived in a beautiful brick home. They must have been rich because they even had hired help. They told Mrs. Bliss that they wanted to have a son…and I was to be that son.

They were very nice to me, and didn't make me do any work. I would wander around the farm, just having fun. I tried not to do anything wrong, and everything was going fine for the first few weeks…fine that was, until I decided to round up a few chickens and, for some strange reason, hid them under a couple of wash tubs.

"I heard someone put the chickens under the tubs," Mrs. Birch said later that day. "Might you know anything about that, Homer?"

I was afraid to tell the truth for fear they would send me back to the home, so I lied. "No, Ma'am. I don't know anything about that."

But they knew I was lying and the next day, Mr. Jenkins was driving me back to the orphanage. I felt pretty ashamed, and didn't have too much to say.

"Cat got your tongue, Homer?"

I shrugged.

"What happened this time?"

"I lied," I whispered.

"Ah," he sighed. "Telling the truth is hard sometimes but

wouldn't it have been easier in the long run?"

"I know that now, but I was afraid if they found out that I hid the chickens, they'd punish me."

"Did they?"

"No, they just said they couldn't trust me anymore because I lied. I don't think I'll ever get adopted."

"Don't give up hope, young man," he said, putting his arm around my shoulder. "Someone's looking for a nice boy like you. You'll see. You're going to have a mother and father real soon."

I wanted to believe him, but at this point, it seemed doubtful I would ever be adopted.

It was right about the time when I was sent back to the orphanage for the second time, that Mrs. Bliss called the school to see how I was doing. Shocked to learn that I had never even been enrolled, she was very upset and I was not allowed to play outside with the other children for the remainder of the school year.

"And in addition to that, Homer," she said sternly, "you will make all the beds every morning for punishment."

"But there's so many," I said, almost in tears.

"That's right, young man. Make every single bed and make them neat. This should teach you a lesson not to play hooky."

I wanted to squeal and tell her that the older boys wouldn't let me go to school, but I remembered their threatening promises, and decided to keep my mouth shut and accept the punishment.

One day, after I finished making the beds, Mrs. Bliss

JOHN BRAUCHT

brought me into her office and told me she was going to put my picture in the newspaper. "Do you have an objection, Homer?"

"Why?" I asked.

"So you can get adopted," she said.

"No," I said. "I don't have any objections. I'd like that."

She showed me a recent photograph of myself, and read the caption beneath it. "How would you like to go fishing with this little boy?"

Little did I realize how that picture would change the course of my life.

A LIFETIME WORTH REMEMBERING

"THE POP-UP TOASTER DEBUTS IN AMERICA"

Chapter Four
1926

It was in August when Georgia Marie Braucht and her husband saw my photo and story in the paper. She immediately contacted Mrs. Smithers, Mrs. Bliss's assistant, and made arrangements to meet with me a few days later. Mrs. Smithers took me to the train station in Waco, Texas, where I was introduced to the woman who would become my true mother for the rest of my life.

"Hello Homer," Mrs. Braucht said, bending down to kiss my cheek. "I saw your photograph in the newspaper and my husband and I thought it would be very nice to go fishing with a little boy like you."

I immediately liked her. She had a kind face that lit up when she smiled. "I'd like that fine, Ma'am," I said politely.

"Well then, that's just fine. And how about you and I going to see a picture show until the train comes?"

I remembered how frightened I was at the last picture show, when I hid in the lobby to get away from the loud thundering noises, but I didn't want her to think I was a sissy, so I said, "That would be very nice, thank you."

We said good-bye to Mrs. Smithers, and walked down the street hand in hand.

"You know, Homer," Mrs. Braucht said. "My husband and I live in Lueders right next to a limestone quarry."

"What's a quarry?" I asked, never having heard the word before.

"Well, the best I can describe it is, that it's a big rock surface that goes around a small lake. Does that answer your question?"

"Yes," I said, pleased that she took the time to explain it to me.

"And as I was saying, we live near a town called Lueders and your new Daddy's name is Glen and people call me Marie, but I hope that you are going to call us Mom and Dad."

She squeezed my hand and I felt happier than I had in a long time.

By the time we arrived at the theater, the picture had already begun. I was startled to see a small barking dog on the screen that grew bigger and bigger. It seemed to jump out at me and without a word, I turned and ran out of the theater, heading back to the train station.

Marie ran after me, calling for me to come back. Finally, I stopped running and by the time she caught up with me, I was at the station.

"What's wrong, honey?" she asked. "Why did you run away?"

"I was afraid the dog was going to bite me," I admitted. "He was jumping right at me."

"Oh, you poor little thing," she crooned. "Hasn't anyone ever explained that the movies are only make-believe. There's nothing on the screen that can hurt you. It's just a big picture, like in a book, only it moves. So you don't have to be afraid."

There was something about her manner that was comforting. I found her easy to believe and was never afraid to go to the movies after that.

We no sooner arrived, than the train pulled into the station. I could hardly wait to get on board. I had seen pictures of trains before but had never ridden on one.

The trip with my new mother was an experience that I still treasure in my heart. I was filled with anticipation as we pulled into Lueders Station. My new father was waiting with open arms as we got off the train.

"Come here, son and give me a big hug," he said when he saw me.

Suddenly I was swept into his arms and into his heart.

We drove to the quarry in an old truck, with me sitting in the middle.

"We don't have a real house, Homer," Marie tried to explain. "We have to live on the quarry because it needs constant supervision. And all the men who work there live right near us. See there," she said, pointing to what looked like a tent. "They call that a squad tent in the army. You won't mind, will you?"

I wouldn't mind at all. Living in a tent sounded like a lot of fun. When we went inside, Marie showed me my bed off to the corner of the room.

"That's where you'll sleep Homer." She smiled at me, and

added. "And you can call us Mom and Dad, if you'd like."

I nodded. "Yes, Ma'am...I mean... *Mom*. I'd certainly like that real fine!"

My new parents were kind and compassionate, and we bonded immediately. I finally belonged to a family and couldn't have been happier. My only regret was that my brothers weren't adopted with me.

I spent most of the days at the quarry, fascinated with the mining operation. I watched the mules pulling the scoops and remember one old gray that would let out one long, loud bray at exactly noon and refused to budge until his harness was removed. He must have been the leader, because once he stopped working, all the other mules refused to move.

I soon became aware of the quarry operation, noting that it took a span of four horses across and eight-to-ten deep to pull the stone in a flatbed wagon from the quarry to the railroad siding. I wanted to ride on the wagons, but I wasn't permitted. My parents thought it might be dangerous.

Sometimes though, when the big trucks hauled the worthless rubble away, the drivers let me sit next to them and I pretended to drive.

When Dad discovered that I was taking rides with the truckers, he cautioned me about the dangers of strangers, and made me promise never to do it again. He also warned me about the danger of rattlesnakes and how they liked to bask on the sun-warmed rocks.

Dovie, a worker's little girl had wandered into a den of snakes one day and everyone held their breath, until her father carried her to safety. I was very careful where I walked after that.

There was a fresh water spring nearby, filled with black catfish no longer than my fingernail. My Dad built a dam to keep the water from flowing into the quarry.

"Let's go swimming," Dad said one day, as he tossed me a big fat inner tube.

"I don't want to go in the water," I protested, remembering the incident at Breckenridge. "I'll drown."

"Don't be silly, Homer. I'm right here to protect you." With that, he plunked the inner tube and me in it, in the water.

I was shaking and holding on to him for dear life, but he was patient. Soon I grew confidant that I wasn't going to drown, and had a great time for the rest of the day.

Dad wasn't a big fellow. At most he was five-seven or eight but strong and wiry. He lost his right hand the previous year in an accident at the Leander quarry.

I finally got up the nerve to ask him how it happened.

"I was working along side a channeling machine that ran alongside a rail like a train track," he explained. "It was going from one end to another and I wasn't paying attention. I rested my hand on the rail, and the machine cut right trough it. It was my own fault for being careless."

"What happened then, Dad? Did it hurt real bad?"

"To tell you the truth, son, I don't remember much. I must have been in shock. A couple of friends tied a tourniquet around my arm rushed me to the Georgetown hospital—"

"Where your Dad nearly bled to death," Mom interrupted. I could see the anger in her face, as she recalled the preventable outcome of Dad's accident.

"That doctor was so incompetent," she continued. "He took the tourniquet off too soon." The anger melted into a smile at Dad. "But your Dad was tough and as you can see, he recovered nicely."

"And," I added, "you can do anything anyone else can do."

"Well Homer, if I can't it won't be for lack of trying," he said, ruffling my hair.

Dad's older brother, Dan owned the stone business, and Dad's job was to develop the new quarries and trouble shoot where and whenever he was needed. When he had to go to a finishing plant or a building site for a few days, I missed him terribly.

A LIFETIME WORTH REMEMBERING

Chapter Five
WINTER 1926

We weren't at Lueders very long, before we moved to Barstow, Texas, a small town just east of Pecos. They were opening up a red sand stone quarry to help build an addition for the courthouse in Austin.

Our new home was a small wooden house. It was more like a cabin and nothing to speak of, but I didn't mind. I was satisfied just being with my parents. Everything to me then was an adventure.

There was no drinking water in the house. Dad took me out back and showed me the cistern, which was nothing more that a wooden platform with a trap door.

"All you have to do, Homer," he said, "is to lower the bucket down and draw up the water. But the main thing you have to remember is, always keep the lid on. That is very, very important. Do you understand?"

I nodded. "Yes, Sir. I understand."

Mom, who was always taking in strays, found a little kitten right after we moved in. It had black spot on his nose so we appropriately named him Spotty Nose.

A couple of days later, Mom said, "Homer, I'm real thirsty. Would you please go get some water?"

"Sure," I said, racing out the door. It was the first time I was allowed to go near the cistern and I was anxious to try it out. Lowering the bucket, I slowly drew up the water, then raced back inside the house trying not to spill a drop.

The next morning when Spotty didn't show up for his breakfast, I looked all over the place for him. Later when Dad went to get a drink from the cistern, he discovered Spotty at the bottom.

Horrified, I remembered that I didn't put the lid back on!

"Didn't I warn you about that, Homer?" Dad said sternly. "Not only did the poor cat drown, but now we're going to have to boil all our water."

"I'm sorry, Dad," I apologized, fighting back the tears. "I forgot...but I'll never do it again."

Mom didn't have to say anything. She knew how bad I felt. It took a long time before I got over the guilt of causing Spotty Nose's death.

My parents slept in the rear of the cabin and I slept up front. I thought I had gotten used to the howling coyotes, but this one night, they were howling louder and longer than usual. I couldn't sleep and got up to look out the window. I was shocked to see the shining eyes of a coyote staring back at me. I pounded the window with all my might, but the eyes didn't move. It took me a few seconds before I realized that I was looking at

A LIFETIME WORTH REMEMBERING

the reflection of a florescent alarm clock in the window. I felt pretty stupid and never told anyone what had happened.

Dad said that the Lueders quarry had thinner layers of limestone so the process of loosening stone was different than the process they used at Barstow.

"We use a steam engine to remove the stone," he explained, as we walked around the quarry. "Sometimes we call it a channeling machine and the piston hammers a row of bars that are laid side-by-side until the desired channel that we want is made.

"Back in Lueders they used a large steel rod to drill the holes," he went on. "You know, Homer, something like a crowbar." He pointed to a big machine. "That's called a scallop. It drops the bar against the stone and hand turns it until it reaches the next layer.
See over there. It makes one hole after another until it shapes the size of block we want to remove. And then we blast it loose with dynamite."

"Wow, Dad," I said, excited at the prospect of seeing a real explosion. "Will you take me with you when they blow up the stone?"

He grinned. "I think that can be arranged."

There was a big to-do about some new efficient type of crane that Dad had recently acquired.

"The new crane moved the biggest stones next to that high tower," Dad explained. "But when we put the main beam up, the men refused to climb up the tower to fasten the cables."

"What happened then?" I asked.

"I volunteered."

"But, how could you? I mean you only have one hand."

"I still had the other one, didn't I? And I only needed one good hand to do the job."

Dad was right, and I never questioned his ability again.

By now I was pretty interested in what was going on around the quarry and was always asking questions about how things worked.

"We're using red sandstone for the new addition at the state capital in Austin," he told me one day. "I think we're going to need some extra help. So, Homer, how would you like a job at the quarry?"

"You mean it?" I asked, eager to work with him.

"Of course I mean it. We had heavy rain this week and the water level is too high. I thought you could help pump out the water."

"How can I do that, Dad?"

"You know that hand pump up on top of the quarry?"

I nodded. "Yeah, I know the one."

"Then you know how you pumped the well in the back yard. It's no different only a little harder. You think you can do it?"

"I sure can."

I wasn't paid, but I had the pleasure of accomplishment, which was an important lesson. Mom always said, "Don't expect payment for family chores, just work for the joy of it."

There were few fresh wells and springs in the Barstow area, and most of those dried up fast in the dry season. Dad had to travel about five miles to the water tower at the train stop

A LIFETIME WORTH REMEMBERING

to get a keg of water. It cost a dollar which was a lot of money in those days and you had to carry a canvas bag of water with you to keep the car radiator from overheating, especially if you had any distance to go.

I started school in the fall of 1926, four months shy of my tenth birthday. Since I had no prior education, a decision was made to put me in the second grade with the younger children. I had little difficulty and was a quick learner.

My main problem was the mispronunciation of certain words. I especially had trouble with words that began with 'th', like 'these' and 'those'.

"Try putting your tongue between your teeth and say 'Th'," my teacher instructed me.

She was patient with me, and eventually I was able to pronounce the words correctly.

Mom always had a treat for me when I came home from school. Usually it was bread and butter, or bread and homemade jam. Most of the itinerant worker's were very poor, and their kids ate bread with thick grey lard.

"That looks pretty awful," I told one of the kids when I got a look at his sandwich.

He nodded. "It wouldn't be so bad," he said "if it didn't stick to the roof of your mouth."

I remember one day when my Dad and I were driving home from the quarry. For some reason, he decided to take a different route.

"I have an errand to run, Homer," he said, starting to

slow the car down. "Just cut across that field to the house."

I thought he meant right then and there so I stepped onto the running board. Before he could stop me, I jumped from the car and rolled into a sandy ditch. Luckily nothing was hurt but my pride when he said, "I meant get out after I stopped the car."

"CHARLES LINDBERGH MAKES THE FIRST NON-STOP SOLO FLIGHT ACROSS THE ATLANTIC OCEAN IN 33.5 HOURS"

Chapter Six
1927

It was the second of January when we took a trip to the Pecos City Hall and it turned out to be one of the most important days of my life.

"Are you positive you want to change your name to Braucht?" Mom asked me. "Remember, the adoption is going to make everything final."

It was the day I was waiting for, and I didn't hesitate. "Yes, Ma'am," I said. "I'm positive."

"Do you still want to be called Homer?" my father asked.

We had gone over this before. I had never liked the name Homer. It was the kind of name that kids made fun of.

"No," I said without hesitation. "I still want to be called Johnny."

And it was that day that I, Homer Wade, officially became Johnny Webster Braucht, named after my Dad's father, Daniel Webster Braucht; the name I proudly bear to this day.

When we got home that night, Mom and Dad sat me

down in the parlor.

"You understand now that you are our truly adopted son from now on," Dad explained.

"I understand and I'm really glad."

"We also have more good news for you," Mom added. "You remember Mrs. Bliss at the orphanage? Well, when I spoke to her she told me where your brothers are. She said when you're a little older you can visit them if you want."

"How are they?" I asked.

"Mrs. Bliss said they were doing pretty good and they have good parents who love them."

I often thought of Clyde and Owen hoping that they were as fortunate as me. Now that I knew they were okay I felt relieved.

In the evening, Dad's Aunt Kate baked a big chocolate cake for the adoption celebration. I received a combination birthday and adoption present; a new tool set, which I had wanted for a long time. I couldn't have been happier.

While we were still at Barstow, several of the Mexican quarry workers dropped by the house one afternoon.

"We want to be paid!" they demanded.

"My parents aren't home," I told them. "My father is out of town."

"We don't care," they insisted. "We want our money today!"

I recalled there were some old checks in the kitchen drawer that Dad let me play with. Thinking checks were the same as money, I signed his name on them and handed them out to the workers. When they tried to cash them, they were told the checks were worthless. They were furious, and were back early the next morning, pounding on the door.

"These are no good!" they complained, waving the worthless checks in the air. Dad took a good look at one of the checks and frowned. "What is this?"

"Ask your boy!" someone shouted.

After I explained what I had done, Dad immediately made good the checks.

Later, Mom sat me down and patiently explained what a check was, and how it was meant to be used.

We didn't have bathrooms inside the house in those days, and on one occasion, I had to use the outhouse. It was night time and I always made sure I went in the daylight. I was afraid of the dark but this time, I had no choice. I really had to go bad.

When I opened the back door, I saw something hovering over the house. I slammed the door shut and yelled, there's a giant out there!"

Mom took my hand and walked me outside. "Look Johnny, over there. It's only a shadow from that big old fir tree. See how the wind is blowing it back and forth? That's the giant you thought you saw."

I felt a little stupid and after that experience, my childish fears started to disappear...thanks to Mom's patience and understanding.

By the time the Barstow Quarry was operating satisfactorily, it was time to move on. We had just finished packing, when my Dad said, "Well, Johnny, when we leave here I guess I'm not going to have anything to switch you with but hard thorny mesquite limbs."

He had never taken a switch to me, but thinking he was serious, I gathered a bunch of fir tree limbs and tied them to the fender of the car. Mom and Dad had a big laugh, as they tossed them into the ditch.

It seemed as if we would just get settled, when we'd be off again. This move took us to a stone fabricating plant in Cisco, Texas.

After we moved into the house, Mom had a telephone installed. I had never seen one before. My first introduction to its use came on a day while I was alone in the house. When it rang for the first time, I didn't know what to do. It continued to ring until I picked up what looked like a handle. Thinking that I broke it when it stopped ringing, I immediately put the handle back on the hook. It rang again and I had no choice but to answer it. I held the handle in front of my mouth.

"There's no one home but me!" I yelled, and slammed the handle down.

I was quite perplexed when it rang once again. I slowly picked it up to hear Mom's voice inside the phone, saying, "Johnny, don't hang up. It's me!" For a moment, I couldn't figure out how she got inside. My folks had a good laugh over that incident too.

We weren't at that house long, when Mom adopted a wild cat that we named Tom, and shortly after, a big yellow Persian we called Sunny. It was like they knew she couldn't

A LIFETIME WORTH REMEMBERING

resist anyone who was homeless.

I was enrolled in the third grade for the remainder of the school year. In addition to learning the three 'R's; 'Readin' 'Ritin' and 'Rithmetic', I learned to make paper-mache. The teacher showed us how to tear strips of paper, and mix them with a little flour and food coloring. Then we drew an outline of a state on cardboard, and sculpted the mache to form mountains.

Dad liked taking me to the Cisco plant. He wanted me to learn as much as I could about stone fabrication.

"That's a gang saw up there," he said, pointing to thin metal sheets with knife-like blades that were suspended over large stone blocks. "That saw swings like a pendulum, Johnny. It keeps getting lower until it cuts through the stone. And if we want the stone to be cut in different sizes, we set the blades at different points."

It was a matter of months when we moved into a second floor apartment to be closer to his brother's Tulsa Oklahoma plant, which was having problems.

Dad warned Dan, "You're expanding too fast, Dan. You don't have enough capital and if you don't slow down, it's just a matter of time before you'll go bankrupt."

But Dan didn't listen and later confessed that he regretted not taking Dad's advice.

Dad was away much of the time that summer, and there wasn't much to do around the plant. Mom took me for walks and sometimes we'd go into town to the grocery store.

She had a natural talent for art and could draw or paint

anything. She was an avid reader and read me wonderful stories that stretched my imagination.

The Bible, Jack London, Oliver Curwood and Zane Gray became my friends even though I was still having trouble reading on my own.

Mom also found time to teach me the benefits of saving money.

"There are two ways to make money," she'd say. "You can work for it or let it work for you." Then she'd add, "And always save some for a rainy day."

"What do you mean, let it work for you?" I asked.

"Well, first you have to save some money that you have earned by working for a rainy day. If you put it under your pillow, the money won't grow but if you put it in the bank in a saving's account, the bank will give you interest."

"What's interest?"

"Say you put ten dollars in the bank," she went on. "Then they give you a sort of present and that's called interest. They give you more money, maybe as much as ten percent more, while they use your money to do other things with."

"If they use my money, can I get it out when I want it?"

"Of course," she said. "You'll not only get your money back, but you'll earn an extra dollar in a year. See, that way your money is working for you."

I liked that idea so much that Mom surprised me with a little metal dime bank that was about three inches long and marked in increments of one dollar. It held about five dollars worth of dimes stacked on top of each other. I could see how much was saved by looking through the small openings on the side. It made saving fun and I liked seeing the money grow.

"I think I want to start my own business," Dad said out of the clear blue sky. "I want to relocate and I'm going to look at East Texas and West Louisiana, maybe even as far as the Gulf."

"Why so far away, Dad?" I asked.

"Because we need to find a location where there's not much stone competition," he explained.

"But," Mom said, "there's not very much competition around here."

"We need more than that to be successful. We need to be in a place where the stone business is booming. And there's no opportunity for us to expand here."

"Should we start packing?" I asked.

Mom laughed and Dad shook his head. "Not just yet." He looked at Mom for a moment. "What do you say we first take a little trip to Oswego."

Mom never argued with Dad. It seemed that she understood that this was the life that was cut out for them.

"I was born in Oswego," Mom told me that afternoon while peeling potatoes."

"Oh," I said, taking a seat at the table. "Where did you and Dad meet?"

"In Oswego when we were still children."

"Where's Oswego?" I asked, never having heard of Oswego before.

"In Kansas," she replied.

"Was Dad born there too?"

"No. He was born in Cassville, Missouri and he had seven brothers and sisters and his mother was a teacher, and his father was a professor. Then they moved to Carthage,

JOHN BRAUCHT

Missouri, where his father worked in the quarries."

"Then how did you meet Dad?"

"Later, they moved to Oswego and opened up a monument shop. Dad went to the same school as me, and that's where we met."

"Where's Dad's mother now?" I asked, interested to find out as much as I could about his relatives.

"Your father's mother died when he was only eight and his sister, Vera, raised him."

"And, what about you, Mom? What about your mom and dad?"

She got up and put the potatoes and a roast into the oven and started setting the table. "Well, my parents names are Angela and John Clark. They're your grandparents now, John, and they live on a little farm in Labette. That's in Kansas. My Dad hasn't been too well, so they moved to the farm because country air is good for him."

I would later get to meet those kind and considerate relatives who treated me as if I had been with them all of my life. Grampa Clark grew to be my favorite and I thought he was about the kindest man in the world. 'Sometimes he was too kind,' Grandma would say with a smile.

"One day," she said, "I went out to the barn to milk the cow. But it wasn't there. I looked everywhere but it was nowhere to be found."

"Where was it?" I asked.

"That's just what I said to your Grampa. I said, where's the cow?"

"He said, 'You know the family with all those children

A LIFETIME WORTH REMEMBERING

who moved next to us?' I told him I did and he said, 'Well, they needed milk more than we do, so I gave them the cow.'"

Grampa was always telling me stories about when he was young and about his mother and father.

"We used to live in a small town in Iowa during the Civil War," he said. "My folks always went to church there. But they got mad at my Pa because he refused to take sides, and they wouldn't let him attend services and the towns people refused to do business with him."

"What did he do then?"

"He loaded us up in a covered wagon and took off for the west."

"Wow," I said, "just like Davie Crockett!"

"Yup, something like that I guess. It sure was cold that winter, cold enough to freeze the nose off your face—." He paused a moment, then continued. "And on the way, my brother died of exposure and my Pa caught pneumonia and died."

He swiped his sleeve across his eyes and I imagined that he was remembering his father and brother. He looked so sad, I wanted to cheer him up.

"What did you do after that?" I said.

"Oh, I managed to survive and when I was a young man, not much older than you, John, I worked as a tinsmith."

"What's a tinsmith, Grampa?"

"Just what is says. I worked with tin and metal, made Revere Ware. You know, like pots and pans. And I got pretty good at repairing stuff, especially clocks."

"When did you move to Labette?"

"Ah, now, let me see." He scratched his head for a moment. "Must be all of twenty some odd years ago. I was feeling poorly, and your Grandma thought it would be a good idea to live on a farm and raise all our own vegetables. We started raising chickens and I even tried my hand at bees."

"How did you raise bees? Didn't they sting you?"

He laughed. "No John, you build them a home that's called a hive and the bees raise themselves. Then every once in a while you take the honey."

I admired Grampa and thought he must be the best Grampa in the whole wide world.

Grandma was nice too. One day, she called me in the house and gave me a cookie, still warm from the oven.

"You want some milk to go with that, Johnny?"

I nodded. "Yes, ma'am."

She poured me a glass and sat down at the table. "Tell me about the Indians when you were a little girl, Grandma," I asked, never tiring of the story. It always seemed to please her when I showed interest in hearing about her life.

"A tribe of Indians lived near us," she said. "And sometimes they went into town and drank spirits. It made them go wild."

"And then they'd ride past your house," I'd add. "And you and your Ma and Pa would hide out in the woods."

She handed me another cookie. "That's right, Johnny, and they never caught us. My Ma used to hide me under a big old iron pot in back of the house."

"Are there any Indians now?" I asked.

"Some, but they're peaceful now and they live on Reservations."

My Dad liked to tell jokes. After I told him the story about Grandma and the Indians, he said he had a story too.

A LIFETIME WORTH REMEMBERING

"A rich Indian struck oil on his land and he bought a new car from a dealer. The next day he was back at the dealers wanting to buy another car. The salesman said, 'You just bought a car yesterday, why do you need another one? And do you know what the Indian said, Johnny?"

I shook my head. I didn't have the faintest idea.

"He said, 'I got drunk last night, and I was driving down the road, and a bridge was coming straight at me so I moved over to let it pass.'" Dad started laughing.

I was puzzled and said, "I don't get it."

"He drove right into the river, Johnny... to let the bridge pass by!"

Grampa was very patient and always doing good deeds for other people. I didn't need to be taught *The Golden Rule*. My family lived it.

Mom did what she preached. "Never do anything you will be sorry for later Johnny, and remember, what you do speaks so loud I can't hear a word you say."

"And don't forget, Mom," I added. "Actions speak louder than words."

Our next move was to the house that Dad built as a young man. It was on the outskirts of the north field of my grandparents' farm. We had a chicken coop and an outhouse with its own library; a *Montgomery Ward Catalogue.*

Horseradish plants thrived in the back yard. Mom ground the large tubular roots in the house to make horseradish sauce. The fumes were so strong it burned my eyes and I had to get out in the fresh air. I don't know how Mom was able to stand it.

We didn't have a phone or electricity and the only light came from a gas lantern. My grandparents used kerosene lamps. At first Mom washed clothes in a galvanized tub, and scrubbed them against a rippled wash board until they were clean. Later, Dad brought home a tub with a concave wash board and a handle that pumped the board up and down and tumbled the clothes clean.

"That new contraption there," he said, "is called a washing machine."

In the summer it was easier to get washed up in the river, but in the winter we bathed in the tub. Mom heated the water in an oval shaped copper tub, which covered two burners on the oil stove. The water took about half a day to get hot, was poured into the tub and each of us took turns taking a bath.

It was our first Christmas at Labette, and it was customary to chop down your own tree. So, Dad and I went into the woods and found a beautiful six-foot fir tree. He gave me the axe and let me chop it down. We dragged it home and into the parlor where Dad set it upright on a board held rigid with wires. I got to nail the tree down.

Mom showed me how to make tree decorations.

"Take the colored paper, Johnny and cut them in long strips like this," she said, demonstrating how to do it. "Once we get a whole bunch made, we're going to glue them together and make a chain."

We finished the paper chain, and after we made a big batch of popcorn, Mom got out a bowl of cranberries and an assortment of old buttons. Then she got a needle and a spool of thread and spread everything on the table. "Now we're going to sew all this stuff together."

Mom laughed when I started to eat the popcorn. "Make sure you leave enough for the tree."

We wrapped the popcorn and buttons around the tree and Mom opened a little box filled with small white candles.

"Now comes the exciting part," she said. "But first I want you to go outside and get a big bucket of sand and a pail of water."

"What do we need that for?" I asked.

She took a candle out of the box and secured it to the end of a branch. "We're going to light these on Christmas eve, and we need the sand and water in case of a fire. We should always be prepared for an emergency."

After the last of the candles was attached, we stood back and admired what we had created.

Finally Christmas Eve was upon us and all the candles were lit. I was filled with a sense of pride and accomplishment seeing how beautiful the tree looked.

I fell asleep that night thinking of Santa Claus coming down the chimney and was the first one up at daybreak. I woke Mom and Dad and ran into the parlor.

I could hardly believe my eyes. The first thing I saw under the tree was a bright red wagon, something I always wanted. It was filled with tools and books. Leaning next to the wagon was a scooter and a big box tied with bright green ribbon. I tore open the wrapper to find the best present ever—an Erector Set.

"Thank you, thank you, thank you!" I said, jumping up

and down. I didn't know if it was my parents or Santa Claus who brought the presents, and I didn't care. I was just so happy to get them.

My library today holds many books from my parents and grandparents library.

Springtime came along and along with it, a mangy, sick collie. He was sitting on our doorstep one morning, half starved and was the worst looking animal I ever saw. Mom, with her big heart, took him right in and fed him.

"Let's call him. Tip," she said, pointing to a white spot on his tail.

Dad took Tip out back and gave him a bath in creosote, and with Mom's tender loving care, Tip was nursed back to health and beauty in no time.

Mom and I were rolling little balls of dough that we used for trout bait, when Tip snatched one from the table and swallowed it whole.

Mom laughed and said, "I hope the trout will bite that fast."

Dad had a double-barrel sixteen-gauge shotgun that he used to hunt rabbit and squirrel. My grandparents, who raised most of the food we needed for canning, had dug out a crude root cellar in the back yard to store vegetables. And in case of a tornado, the root cellars were the safest place to be.

We lived about a half-mile from the small town that consisted of two general stores, a makeshift theater, a post office and a creamery.

"The only time that train stops in town is to pick up passengers and freight. Otherwise," Dad told us, "it only slows down just long enough to snatch the mailbag hanging from a pole."

There was a room over one of the stores that was used occasionally for social and civic events. I remember the box lunch socials where the highest bid allowed a gentleman to spend the picnic with the woman who prepared the lunch.

Frances was a girl in my class who I had a crush on. I found out that her box was going to be tied with a yellow ribbon. Making sure that I would have the highest bid, I broke into my bank and took out all my money.

A dollar and fifteen cents won me the company of Frances and her box lunch. A group of traveling black singers entertained us while we ate at the picnic.

Sometimes on Saturday, Frances and I would go to the movie for the price of one nickel. She was a good friend and fun to be with and we remained friends for many years.

Mom made a big chocolate cake for my eleventh birthday. While everyone was singing 'Happy Birthday', Mom told me to cut the cake. I started to slice into it, when the knife hit something solid in the middle. Puzzled, I looked up at Mom, and saw a big grin spread across her face.

"What is it?" I asked.

"Reach in," she said. "And you'll find out."

I dug inside the cake with my fingers and pulled out a little box. I wiped off the cake crumbs and opened it up to find my first grown-up present…a beautiful pocket-watch.

"I really love this, Mom." I said, giving her a big hug. "Now I won't ever have an excuse for being late."

JOHN BRAUCHT

The two-room schoolhouse was a hop, skip and a jump over the train track from our house. It was next to a pond that froze over in the winter and great for ice-skating.

By now, I was in the fourth grade, which shared a room with third and fifth graders. I learned a lot from both grades when they recited their lessons.

History, geography and especially math came easy for me. The teacher would write a math problem on the blackboard and I was the first to solve it every time. But I always had difficulty in spelling and reading. Other than those two subjects, I was a good student.

Sometimes when Dad was away, Mom and I would stay at Grampa Clark's farm. He raised several breeds of chickens of all colors and sizes; the most beautiful were the brown Leghorn roosters. I wasn't there very long before I got into mischief. I discovered little nesting crates that were meant to house only one hen. I wanted to find out how many eggs a hen laid in one day so I closed the doors on all the nesting hens. When I checked later in the afternoon, I discovered two eggs in each crate. I was very excited with my find and couldn't wait to share the news with my family. Mom and Grampa were in the parlor when I rushed in the house.

"I know how many eggs a hen lays in a day!" I shouted. Grampa grinned. "Oh, and just how many would that be?" I unclasped my fist and held out my hand. "See. Two eggs."

Everyone in the room looked at each other and smiled. Especially Grampa.

"And how do you know that?" he said.

"I tried an experiment. I locked the hens in their crates yesterday and today I found two eggs in each one."

"Well grandson, did you check the crates before you locked the hens in?"

"No. Why?" I asked.

"Because if you had, you would have seen that they had already laid one egg. Then they laid another one today. Hens only lay one egg a day. No more no less." He laughed. "But if you can find some that do better than that, I'll buy them all and we'll be millionaires."

Everyone laughed, and I felt a little stupid.

Mom could see that I was embarrassed, and said, "But you tried, Johnny and that's the most important thing. You'll never learn anything if you don't try."

Grampa knew more about chickens than anyone else did in the world. Even the chickens knew it. When he walked among them, they went about their business, but when anyone else set foot near the coop, they squawked and fluttered about.

Grampa's house was fun. The downstairs bedroom walls were papered with newspapers.

"How come you have papers all over your walls?" I asked.

"Back when we moved into the house, we couldn't afford wallpaper, and the newspapers did the job just fine," Mom explained. "I used to lay in bed and your Grandma would read the papers over and over to me." She laughed. "Especially the funnies. So, you see, John, our not so fancy wallpaper helped teach me to read."

JOHN BRAUCHT

The upstairs bedroom where I usually slept had a mattress stuffed with feather ticking. It itched terribly, and I was always looking for an excuse not to sleep on it. One night when my parents were away, I jumped at the chance to stay in the downstairs bedroom.

There was a terrible storm during the night. The thunder and lightning woke me up with a start. Suddenly I heard a loud crack, followed by a clash of shattering glass. My grandparents and I rushed up the stairs and into the bedroom. We could hardly believe our eyes.

A ten-foot tree branch had crashed through the window and landed on the bed right where I would have been sleeping. Shards of glass covered the bed and floor.

"Thank goodness the boy wasn't sleeping here tonight," Grandma said. "He would have been killed for sure."

It was a long time before anyone could coax me into sleeping in that room again, even after they had moved the bed away from the window.

There was a fireplace in the dining room and a four-hole cast iron stove in the kitchen where Grandma stoked the wood that Grampa chopped in small chunks. We cut through the larger trunks with a long cross saw that took two people to operate and we used an ax to chop up the smaller branches.

I was walking outside the house one afternoon, and noticed a space between the ground and the foundation. It had all the aspects of a great fireplace so I gathered a few twigs and some dried grass and set a match to it.

It didn't take my family long to smell the smoke and come running to see what was happening. Mom was first on the scene. She grabbed a bucket of water and doused the flames.

A LIFETIME WORTH REMEMBERING

After everyone calmed down, Mom took me aside. "You're very fortunate that the house didn't catch on fire, Johnny," she said sternly. "And this is going to hurt me more than it's going to hurt you, but I have to teach you a lesson. Fire is nothing to play around with. We could have all been killed."

She grabbed a switch from a nearby maple tree and spanked me for the first and only time in my life.

After the spanking was over, she said, "Promise me that you will never, ever fool around with matches again."

"I promise Ma'am. I won't ever do that again." I felt ashamed that I made Mom spank me. In the past, whenever I had gotten into trouble, she just sat me down and chastised me in a calm way, which hurt more than any spanking.

The fire episode forgotten, Grandma, who was the greatest cook in the world, especially when it came to fried chicken, biscuits, gravy and berry cobbler, asked me to pick some goose berries growing in the back yard.

I picked more than she needed.

"Why don't you sell the rest?" she suggested.

"How Grandma?"

"Just take them around to the neighbors."

I walked from door to door and sold six pints of berries for a grand total of sixty cents.

That experience turned out to be my first lesson in sales and making money.

JOHN BRAUCHT

I was always looking for things to do...and always getting into things that I shouldn't.

There was a shallow ditch in front of the house that filled up with muddy water after every rainstorm. One hot day, I decided that it was a good place to go wading. I took off my shoes, stepped into the water and onto a piece of glass.

It cut pretty deep and Mom was concerned that it could become infected. "This is going to hurt you more than it is going to hurt me, John," she said, as she daubed the cut with iodine. She was right. The iodine burnt like fire.

"I hope this will teach you not to go wading in the ditch again. Don't you know it's filled with broken glass and junk?"

I never went in that dirty muddy ditch again.

"ALEXANDER FLEMING DISCOVERS PENICILLIN"

Chapter Seven
1928

One morning, Mom called me into the kitchen. "Have a seat, Johnny. I have something very important to discuss with you."

She looked very serious and I quickly took a seat at the table. "What's wrong?" I asked.

She smiled. "Don't worry, son. It's good news. How would you like to have your little brother Clyde come and live with us?"

"Yes, Ma'am, I'd really like that," I said, delighted with the idea. "But, I thought he was adopted?"

"Clyde was raised by a Doctor Leep and his wife and they adopted him when he was almost a year old," Mom said. "But they changed his name to Tommy. Anyway, Mrs. Leep couldn't work and take care of him, because her husband died and she had another child and Tommy was getting to be too much for her."

"So you mean his mother doesn't want him anymore?"

"It isn't that she doesn't want him, Johnny. It's just she has her hands full with other things. She has to make a living to take care of their younger child."

I pondered over what she said for a moment, then asked, "Would you ever give me away?"

She saw the fear in my eyes, gave me a hug, then looked squarely into my eyes and said, "Oh no, son. Your dad and I would never, ever think of that. We love you and you're our son for the rest of your life. Do you understand?"

"Yes, Ma'am," I said, feeling relieved.

"I know it's kind of confusing but the important thing, Johnny is that you are now going to have your little brother to play with. How does that sound?"

"It sounds great, Mom."

Shortly after the discussion with Mom, Dad drove to San Antonio and returned with seven-year-old Clyde.

"This is your big brother, Johnny," Dad said, when Clyde and I came face to face.

Clyde didn't say anything.

"Hi Clyde," I said, walking up to him. "You want to see my toys?"

Clyde nodded and followed me into my room. At first he didn't say much, but after a few days he overcame his shyness and fit in like he had been with us forever. I was overjoyed at being reunited with him.

Clyde was crazy about my father and followed him around the house like a puppy. As a result, they became extremely close.

"How would you like to be named after me?" Dad asked

him one day.

"Clyde grinned from ear to ear. "You mean my name would be Glenwood just like you?"

"Yes. But the only difference is that you'd be Glenwood, Junior."

"Glenwood, Junior," he repeated. "I like the sound of that real good."

After the adoption, my brother was known as Glenwood Braucht, Jr. but for some reason, I stuck him with the nickname Bud. I was the only one outside of the family he allowed to call him by that name.

I was always close to my mother but through the years, Bud continued to grow closer to Dad.

It was shortly after Bud came to live with us that the greatest day in my life occurred. We attended Sunday service in a Baptist church just two blocks outside the town. Reverend Cloninger, the pastor was a good friend of my parents.

It was during one Sunday service that a strange and wonderful sensation came over me. At first I didn't know what it was, but then I remembered one of Reverend Cloninger's sermons when he spoke of being called by God. And then I knew what the sensation was.

I rushed home, bubbling with excitement. I could hardly wait to tell my mother about my experience.

"God called me today, Mom," I yelled, as I came running in the door.

Sitting at the table, sewing a patch on a pair of my pants, she turned to me with a surprised expression on her face.

"That's wonderful, son," she said. "Tell me all about it."

I sat down beside her. "I had this wonderful feeling come over me in Church, Mom."

"How did you know?" she asked.

"I don't know," I said. "But God did. I just got this good feeling inside me, like I never felt before. It felt so good I thought I could fly. God called me."

"Well, then Johnny, I think it's about time we get you baptized."

I recalled seeing people getting baptized at the creek once. They got their heads dunked in the water. "But it's too cold out, Mom."

She laughed. "No, son. You are going to be baptized in the church."

Pastor Cloninger baptized me a few weeks later and after the service, I was playing hide and go seek with the kids when I met his daughter, Orpah.

"I was named after Ruth's sister in the bible," she said, whenever anyone asked her about her unusual name.

Whenever we played after service, she always tagged along behind me. One time when we were playing tag, she grabbed me by the shoulders and kissed me on the cheek. It was the first time I had ever been kissed by a girl and didn't know how to react. I must have felt somewhere between liking it, not liking it and embarrassment.

Anyway, Orpah was likable and sweet and our so-called romance never developed into more than a harmless flirtation. We managed to correspond throughout high school and ended when I went into the service.

A LIFETIME WORTH REMEMBERING

I used to swim at the Neosho River, which was just east of Oswego but my favorite place was Roaring River. There was a trout farm spring where the water flowed over a small dam onto a concrete floor where the trout swam. My cousin Dale, Uncle Dan's son, and I tried to catch them with our hands, but we never had any luck. The fish were always faster than we were.

It was evening when we were leaving, and Dad decided to drive across the shallowest point of the ford, which was just below the trout farm. It was a foolish decision, and the car bogged down in the middle of the river.

"What are we going to do now?" Mom asked, as the water lapped at the side of the running board.

Dad scratched his head and looked at his watch. "Well, it's too late now to go for a tow truck. You and the boys find a place on the shore and relax as best you can. I'll stay with the car —."

"But Dad," I interrupted. "What if the dam breaks? You could drown."

"No need to worry, Johnny. The dam won't break," he assured us.

After a sleepless night, Dad waded to shore at the first sign of daybreak and headed for town. He was back within an hour with a truck that towed our car out of the river.

We never let Dad forget his last words, "The dam won't break," when a few weeks later, the dam broke loose and flooded the area.

Another experience Dad wanted to forget was the time he took me fly-fishing. It was a really cold day and Dad, who was always telling me to be careful, slipped and fell up to his neck in the pond.

"I was out of that icy water so fast, my clothes didn't even get wet," he explained, with a grin that spread from ear to ear.

That was one whopper that got a lot of laughs every time Dad told it.

Another time, I waded into the pond until the water was up to my chin. Standing on my toes to keep from falling over, I flailed my arms about and started kicking like crazy. Before I realized it, I was swimming.

A number of Dad's relatives lived in southwest Missouri. One in particular was his cousin, Floyd Henbest who lived in the Ozarks. We visited him and went hunting for squirrels, rabbits and opossums. Every morning, the table was covered with mouth-watering fried potatoes, meat, white gravy and biscuits and honey.

One night, Dad called Floyd and me outside while Bud was getting a sandwich in the kitchen. "Let's pull a joke on Bud," he whispered.

"What kind of joke?" I asked.

"You remember, Johnny? Me an Floyd pulled it on you last year."

I laughed. "You mean when we went looking for snipes?"

Dad and Floyd motioned me to be quiet. "Yeah, and now its Bud's turn."

"Hey, Bud!" Floyd yelled. "You want to go snipe hunting with us?"

A LIFETIME WORTH REMEMBERING

Bud raced outside. "Sure do!" he yelled back.

"Then you stay right by that tree," Dad said, trying to keep a straight face. "We're going into the woods and shoo the snipes out to you. So don't move until you see those snipes coming out."

"Then what do I do?" Bud asked.

"Throw this over them," Dad replied, tossing Bud a gunnysack.

Bud looked puzzled. "What do they look like?"

"Just like any ordinary snipe. About as big as a basketball and just as round."

Bud stiffened. "Do they bite?"

"Not if you grab them fast enough."

We walked a few yards into the woods and hid behind a tree.

Dad started hooting and hollering, "Here snipe, here snipe!" but when he turned around, Bud was practically on his heels.

"I'm afraid of the dark, Dad," he confessed.

Afterwards we let Bud in on the joke and had a good laugh at his expense.

"You have just been initiated into hunting manhood," Dad explained. "From now on, you can pull the snipe joke on your sons."

"I think I'm ready to start the business now," Dad said one morning. "I want to look at East Texas and West Louisiana, maybe even as far as the Gulf."

"Why so far away, Dad?" I asked.

"Because we need to find a location where there's not

much stone competition," he explained.

"But," Mom said, "there's not too much competition around here."

"We need more than that to be successful. We need to be in a place where the stone business is booming. And there's no opportunity for us to expand here."

In February of 1928, just after my eleventh birthday, Dad announced he was opening the new business in northwest Louisiana. Uncle Dan hadn't taken Dad's suggestion not to take on more than he could handle. so now he worked for Dad.

Dad sold the old car and bought a new *Chevrolet* with windows that could be rolled up and down.

It was about a four-hundred-mile drive to Shreveport. The unpaved gravely roads were bumpy and rutted and were especially narrow in the mountains. Steep ravines without benefit of safety railings made traveling dangerous enough in the daytime, but at night the roads were downright perilous.

It was a long trip, and sometimes Dad couldn't drive any faster than thirty miles per hour. Bud and I grew restless and roughhoused in the car to the point where we exhausted our parent's patience.

On this particular trip we left our dog Tip with a good friend. Unfortunately, we were never to see him again. But we did take our pregnant cat. The first night when we pulled off to the side of the road, she jumped out of the car and never returned. We surmised she had her kittens and wouldn't abandon them.

After we arrived at Shreveport, we rented an upstairs apartment on Eustus Street. We no sooner moved in, than

A LIFETIME WORTH REMEMBERING

Mom had Bud and me enrolled in the Barrett School.

"This is our new student, John Braucht," the teacher announced to the class.

"My name is Johnny," I corrected her.

"Don't you think you are too old to be called Johnny?" she said.

"I guess so, Ma'am," I said. And after thinking it over, I had to agree with her.

That night, I asked my parents to call me John, and have been called that ever since.

By the time school vacation rolled around, I was bored and wanted to earn some money. I started looking for things to do and came up with an idea.

Ne-Hi was my favorite drink, especially the cream soda flavor and their bottling plant was only about a mile away. I put an old wash tub inside my red wagon, and went over to the plant.

"I'd like to buy two cases of Ne-Hi," I said.

"That'll be one dollar," the man said. He put the cases in the wagon. "If you bring the bottles back, we'll give you a penny apiece."

I paid him and then rushed over to the icehouse about a block away.

"I'd like to buy some snow," I said, handing the iceman five pennies.

As soon as he filled the tub with the shaved ice, I was ready for business. I walked up and down the street, yelling, "Get your ice cold pop here! Five cents a pop!"

It wasn't long before I was sold out. I discovered that most people wanted *Coca-Cola*, so I decided to expand my business. In those days there were signs alongside the road, that read, "WE DON'T KNOW WHERE YOUR MOM IS, BUT WE HAVE POP ON ICE". I thought the saying would be a pretty good sales pitch, so I printed the slogan on the side of the wagon.

Soda pop came in six ounce bottles, but *Pepsi Cola* had a larger bottle. Everyone was familiar with the jingle, 'Pepsi Cola hits the spot, twelve full ounces, that's a lot. Twice as much for a nickel too, Pepsi Cola is the drink for you.' So I started selling Pepsi Cola too.

Mom noticed that I was limping when I came home. "What's the matter with your feet?"

"Nothing, they just feel tired. I did a lot of walking today."

"Take off your shoes and walk for me," she said.

I kicked off my shoes and walked across the room.

"My goodness John, I never noticed before, but I believe you have flat feet."

As it turned out I did. Mom took me to see a doctor and he prescribed a steel reinforced brace to wear inside my shoe. It seemed to help and I wasn't as tired after walking around all day.

By the time summer vacation came to an end, I had earned enough money to buy my school book and some of my new clothes. Not only did I feel proud that I spared my parents that expense, but I realized that I was capable of seeing an idea through and making it work.

All in all, I felt pretty good.

A LIFETIME WORTH REMEMBERING

Mom bought a new radio and we hovered around at the set listening to the antics of "Amos and Andy", and "Fibber Magee and Molly". Radio introduced me to a new world.

One night, my friend Danny from next door came over to our house to listen to the radio. We sat on the floor, with our ears glued to the radio.

"I wonder how it works?" I said after we shut the radio off. I was intrigued that voices came out of a little wooden machine.

Danny smiled. "Remember what we learned in school about Thomas Edison?"

"Yeah, what about him?"

He scratched his head for a few seconds, and said, "Well, I think maybe we could make our own."

"Oh sure," I said, in a less than convincing tone. "What would we use for parts?"

"Come on over in the morning and I'll show you."

The next morning, Danny and I went inside the old shed in his back yard. He opened up a cigar box and lifted out a small metal housing and a set of earphones. "See that small piece of glass there?"

"Yeah," I said. "So what?"

"Don't be dumb. It's really a piece of crystal."

He handed me the housing and pointed to a long wire attached to a power outlet. "And this is how we're going to make a radio. All we have to do is make contact with the wire and the crystal."

It turned out to be just that simple. At first nothing happened, but Danny continued touching the wire to the crystal in different places...until we heard some music.

We discovered that by touching the wire to the crystal in various spots, we could tune into several stations. The reception wasn't all that great, but it was fun and our experiment worked.

For some reason, our homemade radio decided not to work one day.

"I think the wire has had it," Danny said. "It's no good anymore."

"So, what do we do now?"

"Let's find the outside power line and use that."

After we located the outside line, I said, "We better find the main switch and shut off the power." We looked all around the house and shed and couldn't locate it.

"Well, let's see if it works anyway," Danny said. He no sooner touched the wire to the power line, than he screamed and fell to the ground.

"What happened?" I yelled.

He started to cry. "I just got electrocuted."

I didn't think the wire could give much of a jolt so I decided to give it a try. I felt a mild tingle and proceeded to twist the wires together and our homemade radio worked again.

Electricity didn't scare me that much, but I was smart enough to respect it.

All the kids in the neighborhood went to a Halloween party. We were getting ready to bob for apples, when one of the older kids decided he wanted to make it more interesting. He took the apple out of the tub and dropped in a quarter instead.

"Now comes the real fun," he said, lowering a live wire

into the water. "All you have to do is take the quarter out of the tub."

A couple of the more daring boys tried to put their hand in but jerked it out the moment it made contact with the water.

I wanted that money and when it was my turn, I thrust my hand in and snatched the quarter as fast as I could. I felt a little shock but it wasn't much more than the one I got when I was hot-wiring the radio.

JOHN BRAUCHT

"THE WORST AMERICAN DEPRESSION BEGINS AS STOCK PRICES PLUMMET ON OCTOBER 29TH"

Chapter Eight
1929

We moved to a one-bedroom house on Olive Street, where Bud and I slept on a converted couch in the living room. There were a lot of kids in the neighborhood, and one of our favorite places to play was in a big empty house at the end of the block. It had huge wooden columns, something like you'd find on a plantation.

A bunch of neighborhood boys and me ran around the house shooting at each other with homemade rubber guns. First we carved a wooden pistol, then cut strips from an old inner tube and stretched them from the front to the back of the pistol. I also carved a longer gun out of a one-by-six board and notched it several times to hold several rubber bands at one time. I called this my machine gun.

One day I found a bullet on the street and thought if I pounded on the cap end, it would make a loud noise and shoot straight ahead. It went off, but not as I had expected.

JOHN BRAUCHT

With barely a sound, the cap backfired and struck me in the right leg. It wasn't a serious wound, but it hurt like the blazes.

That day I learned another valuable lesson, "Don't play with bullets."

We had barely finished unpacking at Olive Street, when Mom announced, "This place is too cramped." So then we moved into a two-bedroom house on Robinson Place.

In those days it was considered prudent to save product coupons and the most popular coupons were from *Octagon Soap*. I saved chewing gum foil, and the boy next door saved Octagon coupons. Then we'd swap. It took me about six months to collect two hundred coupons. I sent them to Octagon, and they sent me a beautiful silver-plated tea set, which I gave to Mom on her birthday.

"USING MAGNETIZED PLASTIC TAPE, THE TAPE RECORDER IS DEVELOPED IN GERMANY"

Chapter Nine
1930

Dad's new corporation was called B & B CUT STONE CO. "We chose that name, because of my initials and my partner, Bolton," he told me one day. "Bolton and I pooled all our resources, equipment and money, John. I'm president with 72 percent of the business and Bolton's vice president with the rest. And our attorney's a member of the corporation."

"Now that you're thirteen, John," Dad continued, "how about if I hire you to work at the plant?" He grinned. "And how about if I pay you a salary too?"

I could hardly believe my ears. "That's great, Dad. So what do I have to do?"

"Your job will be to shovel the dust and scrap stone into a wheel barrel and dump it into the ravine. And you have to make sure the floor is always kept clean. We don't want anyone to get hurt."

Dad explained that he was responsible for sales, financing

and drafting, and Bolton's job was to make sure the stone was finished to the architect's specifications.

Bolton did his job well, but he had a couple of bad habits that bothered me. He yelled and swore a lot at everyone.

One day, he got angry and swore at me.

"I quit," I said. "I don't like you or anyone yelling at me."

"I'm sorry, Johnny. But your dad and I are working so hard to make this business a success that sometimes I lose my temper. But you are doing a great job."

I really didn't want to quit. I wanted to prove to Dad that I was responsible and could hold down a job. I thought it over and came up with a solution. "I'll stay, Mr. Bolton, but on one condition."

"And that is?" he asked.

"You have got to stop swearing and yelling at everyone here," I insisted.

"Then I guess I have no choice but to stop swearing and yelling," he agreed.

He was never perfect and sometimes he got angry but he never swore and yelled at anyone again...as long as I was at the plant.

None of Dad's business associates were aware that he neither drank nor smoked. They gave him a couple of cartons of Four Roses whiskey at Christmas time. Dad told me he tossed the cartons of whiskey away in a pile of scrap stone.

When Dad left the plant, I saw Bolton take the cartons, and strain the whiskey through cheesecloth into a pail. I told Dad what I had seen a couple of days later, when I didn't see Bolton around.

"Bolton has a drinking problem," Dad explained. "And he got real drunk around the holidays."

"Is that why he made so many mistakes with the stone?" I asked.

Dad shook his head. "Liquor will do that to some men, so that's why I had no other choice but to buy him out of the business."

JOHN BRAUCHT

"THE GEORGE WASHINGTON BRIDGE OVER THE HUDSON RIVER OPENS, BUILT WITH DOUBLE THE SPAN OF THE PREVIOUS RECORD HOLDER"

Chapter Ten
1931

It was during the midst of the depression when Dad decided to start a new business making tombstones.

The stock market crashed in '29 and over 20,000 people committed suicide. Later, President Herbert Hoover would announce that the banking system of the United States had collapsed. People were hungry and out of work. World War Veterans had been returning home for ten years with no homes to go to, and industry as a whole was almost at a standstill.

Will Rogers joked that we were the first nation to go to the poor house in an automobile.

It was the worst time for anyone to be starting a new business, but Dad was determined to do just that…and when Dad made up his mind, nothing could stop him.

The only problem was that all the banks were closed and Dad needed a loan. Fortunately, Mom had a degree of foresight. She withdrew her money just before the banks went bankrupt and I had a little money saved.

"We want you to take this money, Glen," Mom said. "It's not much, but I think it's enough to get you started."

Dad was a very proud man and at first he was reluctant. "If I do, then it's got to be a business deal. Okay?"

"Sure," Mom said. "Anything you say."

"I'll pay you back with ten percent interest."

Mom started to interrupt, but Dad silenced her with, "Or it's no deal."

That is how Mom and I came to help Dad start the Braucht Stone plant.

Dad took me over to a vacant open-air structure on McNeil Street, which was located adjacent to a commercial railroad siding.

"They built it this way, John," he explained, "because breathing stone dust is dangerous. Nowadays, the stone cutters have to wear masks, but before they didn't have to."

"What happened to them, Dad?" I asked.

"They developed lung disease."

"We'll be ordering thick slabs that will fill most of the requirements."

"You mean like trim and windowsills," I added.

"Right. Then they go to the cutter's benches."

We continued walking around the plant, with Dad explaining every detail. He pointed across the street to the railroad siding.

"See over there," Dad said. "See those flatbeds. That's where the large stone slabs will come in on."

"How do they get them to the plant?"

A LIFETIME WORTH REMEMBERING

"Big crowbars, rollers and cranes."

As soon as the plant was in operation, Dad installed an electric crane in place of the old hand-operated one. This not only saved on time, but saved on manpower as well.

Then, Dad's next move was to buy a black diamond toothed saw.

"That twenty-four inch saw does a faster and a smoother job," he said.

Linwood Cobb operated the saw and taught me many things at the plant. Every once in a while, I'd make a mistake.

"Remember, John," he would say, "You're gonna learn more by makin' mistakes. If you don't try, you don't learn nothin'. It takes courage to make mistakes."

I remembered his words well, and must have had a lot of courage during my life.

As I grew older and stronger, I took on many different jobs at the plant, and knew the operation from beginning to end.

One day a hard-working black man and I were lifting a heavy stone block. I was doing the same amount of work, but he was more experienced and got twenty-five cents an hour, which was fifteen cents more than I got.

In the summer I worked ten-hour days from Monday through Friday, and five hours on Saturday, which earned me all of five dollars and fifty cents a week.

Stonecutters were the highest paid in the plant since it took years to become a journeyman. Their pay ranged from one dollar to four dollars an hour.

By the end of the first year, Dad's business was doing well. He had long paid back the debt to Mom and I, with interest. He even gave us a bonus when he was contracted to furnish the stone at Barksdale Air Field.

Several columns around a tower had to be turned by a lathe, then squared at the top and bottom. I was only making thirty-five cents an hour doing the same job as the stone cutters who were making a dollar an hour.

"I can do the same job as the cutters in half the time," I told the supervisor.

He watched me work for the rest of the day, and seeing that I proved my point, had no choice but to give me a raise. I was now making all of fifty cents an hour.

I sawed the stone blocks to the exact sizes and shapes for the planer, stone cutter and lathe operator. The draftsmen then cut a precise pattern from tin to make sure the exact specifications were adhered to.

One day, the chain that set the speed and caused the blade to move through the stone, slipped off the gear drum. I thought I could fix it. I held the chain over the first notch, and set the gears in motion. It worked perfectly but I did not take my hand away quickly enough and the blade took the tip off my middle finger. I didn't tell anyone. I held my hand in some ice until it stopped bleeding, then wrapped it in a handkerchief.

I was afraid to tell my parents and tried to conceal my injury by keeping my hand in my pants pocket. By the time Dad noticed my bandaged hand, several days had passed.

"Why didn't you tell me sooner?" he asked on the way to the doctor's office.

"I didn't want you to know that I was careless," I said. "I was ashamed."

"You should be more ashamed to keep it from us. Remember, I was careless too when I lost my hand, so I'd be the last one to criticize you."

"It's a wonder you don't have an infection," the doctor said, shaking his head in amazement.

"Is it going to be okay?" Dad asked him.

"Oh, sure. And as a matter of fact, John was fortunate. He only lost the tip before the first joint."

I laughed. "I don't think that was fortunate."

"Well, you should," the doctor added. "You're young enough that there's a good chance that your finger will grow back again."

And I was fortunate. The tip did grow back.

As the depression worsened, some of the men who rode the rails would come to the house asking for food. Mom would always see that they were fed.

Dad told me that when he was a young man, he rode the rails for a while.

"I wanted to see the country," he explained. "And I didn't have any money so I'd hop a ride on a box car, and straddle the rods under the car. Every time I needed money, I'd hop off the train and harvest the wheat fields. I guess I stopped at most of the farms from Texas to Canada."

"Why did you stop," I asked, envious of his adventurous life.

"Because of all the fumes, and dust and cinder that got

into my lungs, not to mention the danger of getting killed. I'm fortunate I don't have any permanent damage."

I wasn't so envious when I heard the downside of traveling the rails. Yet, I wondered what it would be like to see the world.

Little did I know then, what fate would hold in store for me?

While I was in the fifth grade at the Creswell School, I was expected to memorize a poem within an hour and recite it. We were seated alphabetically and I was one of the first called. I stood up and started to recite, but I was nervous and stumbled over the words.

"Go to the cloakroom, John," the teacher said. "Perhaps you can remember the rest of the poem while you're there."

By the time the rest of the kids had finished reciting, the teacher called me. "You can come out now, John."

She was surprised to find that I was able to recite the entire poem without making a mistake. I can remember the words to this day. I walked to the front of the class, and cleared my throat.

"This poem is called, *Opportunity*, I said. "It was written by 'Anonymous' and it goes like this:

> This I beheld or dreamed it in a dream
> There spread a cloud of dust along a plain
> And underneath this cloud or in it raged a furious battle
> Men yelled, sword shocked against sword and shield.
> A prince's banner wavered then staggered hemmed by foe
> A craven hung around the battled edge and thought
> If I had a sword of keener steal that blue blade the king's
>   son bears

A LIFETIME WORTH REMEMBERING

But this blunt thing
He snapped and flung it from his hand and snuck
  away and fled
Along came the king's son wounded weaponless
  and sore bested
Saw the broken sword hilt buried in the dry and
  sodden sand
He ran and snatched it and with a battle shout lifted
  afresh
And hewed his enemies down and saved a great cause
  that heroic day

When I became a man, I visited fifth grade classes as often as possible and spoke on the importance of memorizing.

JOHN BRAUCHT

"AVIATOR AMELIA EARHART IS THE FIRST WOMAN TO FLY ALONE ACROSS THE ATLANTIC, FLYING FROM NEWFOUNDLAND TO IRELAND IN 13.5 HOURS"

Chapter Eleven
1932

Our next move was to an even bigger house in Stephenson. I was now thirteen and admired an older girl. Mildred Crow was a star tennis player. One afternoon she called me aside and asked, "How would you like to carry my rackets to the courts, John?"

I was surprised and honored that she would ask me and managed to mumble, "Yeah, sure."

I carried her stuff any time I had a chance and was the envy of all my friends.

When I wasn't working or in school, I'd hunt for crawfish at night with a bunch of my friends. The crawfish were easy to find because they left a hole in a small mound of mud and we'd reach in and pinch their claws together.

It was during this time that we played scrimmage ball at Betty Virginia Park. My talent lay in pitching. Throughout my life, when it came to playing ball, I was always the pitcher. I played football for a while, but that sport came to an abrupt end when I injured my tailbone and broke my nose. In grammar school, my first love was track and field sports and I particularly excelled in the broad jump.

I became a Boy Scout when we lived on Olive Street, and was awarded a merit badge. I was real proud of it and couldn't wait to show it off.

"See what I got," I said, holding the badge out in front of a friend.

He snatched it out of my hand and stared at it. "What's this piece of junk?"

"It's an award. It's my second class badge," I said proudly. "I got it from the Boy Scouts."

He flung the badge into a grassy field and with his hands on his hips, said, "So?"

I searched for it in the field while he ran away. I could still hear him laughing as I searched for the badge. After a while I gave up. The grass was too thick and too high. I didn't understand why he did such a mean thing. Ironically, he became a minister years later.

I told Mom about what happened. "He's jealous, she suggested. Later, when I earned my first class badge, I wanted to show it off but thought better of it.

I was a member of the Boy Scout's drum and bugle core. Although I had been given a bugle at Christmas, I knew nothing about music. The scout leader taught us to play by reading notes, but we learned more by listening and playing along with the teacher.

A LIFETIME WORTH REMEMBERING

By now, I saved enough money to buy a bicycle. I had my eye on a sturdy looking one called the Black Beauty for a long time. I paid cash because my mother taught me never to buy anything on time.

"It will cost you more in the long run," she said, "because of the interest."

I loved riding the Black Beauty, especially since I paid for it with my own money, which made it seem all that more important to me. I was riding on the street, along with the traffic one afternoon, when a truck pulled out of an alley directly in my path. I hit the brake, leaned on the pavement for balance and the truck ran over my foot. It didn't hurt too bad, but when I told my mother what happened, she rushed me to the doctor.

"You are a very fortunate young man that your foot wasn't broken and I guess this is the reason why." He took the steel brace out of my shoe and smiled. "This must have cushioned the weight of the truck. But you have very little arch to your feet."

He was right. Years later, when I tried to enlist in the Navy, I was turned down because of flat feet.

The house on Stephenson eventually proved too small for my family, which now included Mom's parents, Bud and me, so we moved to West Kerby. The house was at the end of the block and backed into an open field and woods.

I enrolled in Byrd High School, which was a couple of miles from the house. On my way to school, I passed a Mexican who was selling hot tamales from his two-wheeled cart. They were delicious and whenever I had some extra money, I'd buy one.

"That old Mexican guy kills cats and dogs and grinds them up and cooks the meat like hamburg," one of the kids in school told me one day.

I suspected it was nothing more than a rumor, but it killed my appetite for Mexican tamales for quite a while.

Grandpa raked a huge pile of leaves in the back yard and set a match to it. A sudden gust of wind swept the fire across the field. Everyone in the house ran out when they smelled the smoke. They managed to stomp it out in minutes with wet gunnysacks.

A young neighbor, who would later write a story about her return to Shreveport and what became of her childhood friends, helped us put out the fire. She prophesized that I would become a taxi driver. She was partially right. I later taxied planes around the world.

That year, the drama club produced a play adaptation of the *Legend of Sleepy Hollow*. I wanted the role of the headless horseman, Brom Van Brunt, but didn't get the part and ended up as one of several actors dancing the "Virginia Reel". My mother made my costume and put buckles on my shoes. As a result of that play and that costume, I decided never to be an actor.

I was about fourteen when I started going steady with Katherine Goodwin. I wanted to be with her all the time and didn't have eyes for anyone else.

"Will you go to church with my parents and me tomorrow?" Katherine said one Saturday morning.

A LIFETIME WORTH REMEMBERING

"Sure," I said.

"Then come over to my house tomorrow about six."

I couldn't wait to see her and it was the first time she wanted me to go with her parents. I was just about to ring the bell, when Katherine opened the door and stepped outside.

"I don't have to go to church tonight," she whispered. "Let's go to the movies instead."

"Well I guess that will be okay," I said reluctantly. I knew that if my parents found out I didn't go to church they'd be upset. Not only that, I hadn't planned on going anywhere that was going to cost money.

"But I only have a quarter and the adult tickets are fifteen cents apiece. And we're both over twelve."

"Don't worry," she said. "I know a way to get in."

When we got to the Singer Theater, she stood to the side of the building. "You go over there and get one adult ticket for yourself, and one child's ticket for me. Tell them I'm only twelve."

We got into the movie for twenty-five cents, and that was the first and last time I ever let her talk me into doing anything dishonest again.

We continued dating for about a year until she met the high school football star...and that was the end of that relationship.

JOHN BRAUCHT

"ADOLF HITLER IS APPOINTED CHANCELLOR OF GERMANY"

Chapter Twelve
1933

When I was a freshman, I started hanging around with Paul Goodman who had a very pretty older sister. Marjorie Goodman never paid me much attention.

"My sister jumps out of planes," Paul bragged, while we were watching a baseball game. "And she's not afraid of anything."

I never knew anyone, let alone a girl, who was such a daredevil. Marjorie intrigued me.

One day, when I was at Paul's house, Marjorie said, "John, my car broke down. Do you think you could drive me to the airport?"

I couldn't say 'yes' fast enough. It was an unexpected and welcomed opportunity so I borrowed Dad's car and ended up getting to know her better. After that, I spent most of my time at Marjorie's house and felt honored when she allowed me to run her errands and take her places. All the while, I was developing a big crush on her.

The crush came to a sudden crash when I discovered she was going out with a guy who had a better car than I did. So, that was the end of that relationship.

Later that year, I felt a strong desire to see my younger brother Owen who I figured had to be about thirteen years old by now.

"I'd really like to see my brother, Owen," I told Mom. "Do you think we can find him?"

Mom was sympathetic and understood how I felt. "I'll call the orphanage. They should know something."

The next day, Mrs. Bliss was kind enough to give Mom a phone number. "He's living with a Mr. & Mrs. Lay as far as she knows."

I was eager to talk to Owen. "Can we call right away?"

Mom handed me a piece of paper with the number on it. "Yes, Johnny and I think it should be you to make the call."

I dialed, and the phone rang a few times before a woman answered.

I was nervous and took a deep breath. "Hello, is this Mrs. Lay?"

"Yes," she answered. "And who is this?"

"My name is John Braucht and Owen is my younger brother. And the reason I'm calling is I wonder if it would be all right with you if we could get together? I haven't seen him since we were little kids and I miss him."

"Oh my goodness!" she exclaimed. "I remember you. I wanted to adopt you, too…but wasn't your name Homer then?"

"Yes Ma'am, but I changed it to John when I got adopted."

"I see," she said after a long pause. "May I speak with your mother, John?"

I put Mom on the phone and after she explained the situation, Mrs. Lay said she'd get back with us.

A few weeks later, I received the long awaited call. "I explained everything as best I could to Owen," Mrs. Lay said. "He was really upset to find out he had two brothers and nobody told him. He stayed in his room for days and refused to talk to us."

I felt bad for Owen. It must have come as a shock to him. "Is he okay now?" I asked.

"I think so," Mrs. Lay said. "He thought things over and now he's looking forward to meeting you. He knows it wasn't your fault."

"That's great!" I yelled. "Tell him I'm coming to see him as soon as I can."

In less than a week, I had a round trip bus ticket to San Antonio and was on my way. It was late when I arrived, and I didn't want to disturb the Lays, so I took a room at a local hotel.

I called them first thing in the morning, and they immediately came to the hotel where I was waiting in the lobby.

I knew as soon as Owen walked through the door that he was my brother. He walked toward me and Mrs. Lay held back. I wanted to hug him but was brought up to think that men did not hug each other. Instead, I reached out and shook his hand. "Hi Owen," I said nervously. "I'm your brother Johnny."

He grinned. "I know. My mother told me."

It was an awkward but an impressionable meeting, though I was disappointed that we didn't look alike. We spent the next few days getting to know each other better.

We played ball, fished and went to the movies. We laughed and had a lot of fun together. The awkwardness completely disappeared and we bonded. Twelve missing years melted away.

After I returned from my reunion with Owen, I started high school and Byrd High turned out to be a rewarding experience. I was athletic, and even though I wasn't too tall, I tried out for basketball and became fairly good at jumping center. I practiced with J. Linsey who was considered the best center our team had. His father owned a classy *Pierce Arrow* automobile. Linsey was allowed to drive to out-of-town games, always took me along.

The car had been modified so that the muffler could cut in or out. As soon as we were in the country, Linsey would cut the muffler and we could be heard a mile away. Riding in that car made us the envy of all the kids and it didn't hurt us with the girls either.

Basketball was fun, but it was not my best sport. I always liked to run, so I tried out for track and excelled in it. The two men to beat were Gus Demopulus on the mile and Maston Powel on the half-mile. Try as I might, I never beat either, always coming in second.

In our senior year, Gus, Maston, myself and a guy named Peter competed in the mile relay for state championship. We won and set a new state record. After graduation, Maston, Gus and I ran the fastest time in the mile and half mile events.

One evening, when I was wandering around the neighborhood, I spotted a vacated house. I was curious and decided to see if anything was left inside. The door was unlocked and I went inside. It was as clean as a whistle. In those days it was considered a disgrace if you moved and didn't leave the place spotless. I walked around the house checking every nook and cranny, and discovered a small revolver hidden on the top shelf of a kitchen cabinet. When I reached for the gun, it went off and a bullet passed clean through my thigh. Surprisingly, there was no pain even though my leg was bleeding profusely. I carefully replaced the gun, and stumbled home.

Dad applied a tourniquet to stop the bleeding and called the doctor. I was very fortunate that I had no permanent damage to my leg and needless to say, I learned a valuable lesson about guns and to stay out of other people's property.

JOHN BRAUCHT

A LIFETIME WORTH REMEMBERING

"SHIRLEY TEMPLE STARS IN THE FILM 'BRIGHT EYES' AND SINGS 'ON THE GOOD SHIP LOLLIPOP'"

Chapter Thirteen
1934

After Grampa died, we moved to Dixie Gardens. Work was hard to come by as the country was still in the midst of the depression. We always had enough to eat, since we raised our own food on the farm. We were fortunate but a lot of people were not.

Bud got into an argument with a boy sitting in front of us on the school bus.

"If a black man leaves our plantation and he owes us money," the boy bragged, "we get the police to catch him and they beat him up and sometimes they even shoot him."

"That's rotten and mean," Bud said angrily. "Blacks are human beings. They're not slaves."

"Who cares," the boy snarled. "Blacks are like animals."

"No they're not. They're nice and some of them even work for my father."

"And my Dad pays them good money too," I added, taking Bud's side.

"Aw, you guys are jerks," the boy said and turned his back on us.

I personally witnessed one brutality. When Dad and I were driving along the highway, we saw a group of white men poking a black man with sticks, who was tied to a tree. Dad stopped the car and got out.

"What's going on," he called to the men.

"He insulted a white woman," one of the men shouted back. "You mind your own business!"

"Has he been to trial?"

"He don't need no trial. We know he did it. So if you don't want any trouble, you better get back in your car and get out of here fast."

Dad had no choice but to get back into the car and drive off.

The depression was especially difficult for the blacks. I remember Mary, an elderly black woman who came to our house looking for work.

"What kind of work do you do?" Mom asked.

"I does a little dustin'," she said. "But I sure does need to work."

Mom felt sorry for her, just like she did the strays she took in. "I can't pay you very much, Mary."

"I doesn't care. I does it jest for food."

"Well," Mom said, "I think we can give you a little bit more than food."

Mary turned out to do a lot more than 'a little dustin'." She was very conscientious and trustworthy, and helped Mom out in many, many ways while she was with us.

A LIFETIME WORTH REMEMBERING

Dad employed two talented black men at the plant. Rufus and his very artistic son J.T. designed magnificent ornaments, with delicate chiseled flowers and intricate designs on the tombstones. J.T. was also a master craftsman in setting marble in buildings and I was proud to be his assistant. I remember one rush job that was too big for J.T. and me to handle, so Dad contacted the union to send over some marble setters. When the men arrived at the construction site, they took one look at J.T. and refused to work with him.

Dad's small frame stood tall as he faced the men. "Well, if you think I'm going to fire this man," he said, "you are dead wrong. And you can go find work elsewhere. That is if you can find work elsewhere."

Dad knew what he was doing. The men grumbled among themselves for a few minutes, then reluctantly decided to go back to work.

Though no longer slaves, it was almost impossible for black workers to make a decent living. Their employers gave them a shack to live in and forced them into using credit at the company store. As a result, they were constantly kept in debt.

Our family felt sorry for the blacks and Dad gave work to as many as he could.

I'd always known that I could do anything I wanted…IF I wanted to do it badly enough. And so it was that I decided to pick cotton and earn some extra money during summer vacation.

Dad was out of town at the time, so I asked Mom and she gave me permission.

JOHN BRAUCHT

I got the job and started work the next morning at daybreak. I was surprised to see that all the cotton pickers were black.

It was back breaking work but the blacks never complained. They kept their spirits up by singing throughout the day. It almost made cotton picking enjoyable... if that were possible but I was exhausted by the time I got home.

The weight of cotton in the morning was heavier than the evening weight because of morning dew. The more pounds picked, the more money they earned, so most of their energy was spent working in the morning.

The workers were expected to buy their groceries from the store that was owned by the cotton company, and their bill would automatically be deducted from their pay. That procedure, plus the fact that they were not allowed to purchase groceries elsewhere at more reasonable prices, kept them in debt. Slavery might have been abolished, but in those days it certainly was not dead.

When Dad returned from his trip and learned that I was working from morning until dusk, he was upset.

"I don't want you working those hours—"

"But, Dad," I interrupted, "I don't mind."

"No John. You don't need money that bad."

"Can I at least finish the week then?"

"Just for the week. Understood?"

By the time the week was over, I was glad that Dad had made me quit.

At eighteen, I enlisted in the National Guard, and a couple of months later, joined Junior ROTC in high school.

A LIFETIME WORTH REMEMBERING

The Guard assigned me to the 156th Infantry, and every weekend we trained in the Armory, which was in the basement of the courthouse.

I was listening to the radio the night that Huey P. Long was shot and killed.

"All members of the 156th Company E, report immediately to the Armory," the announcer said.

I reported that evening, and the commander of our unit told us, "We're going to Baton Rouge. It looks like there could be trouble there, and our job is to keep the peace and order."

Two days later, we lined up in front of a large crowd gathered at the foot of the courthouse steps in Baton Rouge. Many people protested against what they perceived to be crooked politics while others defended the politicians.

The day that I was on duty, we were seen as a deterrent to violence, and the crowd dispersed without incident.

Later that summer, our unit was ordered to Camp Beauregard, in Alexandria, Louisiana, for light training which consisted mostly of close order drill, field trips, and target practice for one week. I was assigned to Company "E", with Company "F" marching behind us, singing songs with new verses added each year.

Byrd High, Junior ROTC was assigned a cavalry Colonel, who at one time had been in the Swiss army. He always wore regulation cavalry boots and carried a crop that he slapped against the sides of his boots.

I owned a similar pair of boots, and they were difficult to get on and off. I used a hook to pull the boots on, but getting them off wasn't as simple. The easiest way was to slip your booted foot between the legs of someone facing away from you and have them grab the heel. You then placed your other foot on their rump, gave a gentle push, and off came the boot.

An army sergeant who did the personal work with the volunteer students was assigned to our unit. I hung around him so much that he decided to let me work with him. My job was to measure each student for uniforms, which later helped in my being promoted to captain.

Fair Park was a nearby high school that also had a Junior ROTC Unit. Both units met at Byrd's Stadium to compete for the Best Drilled Cadet. Brass from the Army supervised the competition. One by one, cadets were eliminated until I was the only one left. After a ceremony, I was awarded a medal with a ribbon, and to my surprise, Dad did the honors by pinning the medal on me. It seems only right since he was the Post Commander of the local *Veterans of Foreign Wars* who had furnished the medal.

"CHARLES RICHTER DEVELOPS THE RICHTER SCALE, USED TO MEASURE THE STRENGTH OF AN EARTHQUAKE"

Chapter Fourteen
1935

When we were living in Dixie Gardens, Mom told me that when she and Dad decided to get married, one of the first things Dad bought was a desk. The six-foot tall secretary, as it was called, had three framed mirrors and drawers that could be locked. It opened up to make a desktop, with several small cubbyholes for letters and small items.

I was allowed to keep my most important possessions inside one of the drawers. One was a loose leaf binder in which I kept a record of the top ten songs from the "Hit Parade", clippings from *Ring Magazine* about top boxers in their weight divisions that I pasted in a notebook; a record of my school functions and letters from my friend, Orpah.

Years later, after I had left home, Bud took over the desk and burned all my things but Orpah's letters. Some of the stamps on the envelopes proved to be valuable, and I donated them to a religious charity.

We had a garage in the back yard and I decided to go into the chicken and egg business. I bought some metal cages on rollers, which were called batteries. Next I bought a couple hundred day-old chicks. Most of them turned out to be roosters, which I sold. I built roosting houses for the hens and when they began laying, I marketed the eggs to stores and from house to house. It was a successful and profitable first year as I raised over a thousand egg laying hens.

There was one big Rhode Island Red rooster named Alexander the Great, who followed me everywhere around the farm. One day, a friend of mine brought his little Bantam over to the house.

"I bet my rooster can whip your rooster," he challenged me.

Alexander was young and his spurs just nubs but he was big and I figured he could easily beat the puny little Bantam.

"I don't think he can," I said. "My rooster can take him in a minute."

We put the two roosters face to face. The little Bantam strutted up to Alexander, puffed up his feathers and chased my little coward all around the yard.

Alexander was not so great after that experience, and I learned never to judge anyone by his size again. I compared that contest to the story of David and Goliath.

We had a Jersey cow named Blackie and a Guernsey named Red. Red was definitely head cow in the 'pecking order' of cows. Whenever a neighbor's cow wandered into our pasture and headed toward Blackie, Red was always there to protect her, by nudging the intruder away.

A LIFETIME WORTH REMEMBERING

Prince was a young farm horse that we used to plow the fields. When the corn was ripe it grew so tall, that I had to ride Prince through the rows in order to pick it.

The cattle grazed on the west side of the farm and we grew Irish and sweet potatoes, some as large as a man's head, on the east side.

To keep the cows fresh with milk, Mrs. O'Hara, our neighbor who looked to me, about ninety-years old, led them to the bull to be bred and sometimes this proved to be no mere task. The young heifers were sold or butchered before they reached maturity.

We bought a pig from a nearby farm. Puggy, as we named him, was very smart and easier to train than a dog. But he had a stubborn streak. Puggy continuously managed to dig free from his sty, and raced back to his old farm. I then would have to carry a disgruntled and squealing Puggy home over my shoulder. It was several months before he decided to stay with us.

The dreaded day finally came when Puggy was big and old enough for butchering. By now, he was more of a pet to the family...but a pet we couldn't afford to keep.

The man who did all our butchering was aware that we were reluctant to kill Puggy.

"I assure you he will feel no pain," he said convincingly.

I was not quite convinced, but I wanted to believe him.

After Puggy was reduced to pork chops and ham hocks, we couldn't bring ourselves to taste a mouthful and Dad donated Puggy's remains away to a needy family.

Hard work was not Bud's cup of tea, but one day he surprised everyone by saying, "I want to milk the cows."

Dad cocked an eyebrow. "Are you sure, Bud? That's a big responsibility."

"Yeah, I'm sure."

"You've been around here long enough to know how important it is that they have to be milked twice a day."

"I know that, Dad."

"And you have to make sure the bags are empty," Mom added. "If you don't the milk will dry up."

"I know, Mom," he said.

"Then I guess you got the job. You never learned to milk the cows, John," Dad said, looking at me.

I knew that Bud wanted the opportunity to feel important and responsible. He milked the cows faithfully and I'm sure he felt a sense of accomplishment.

Dad never had a problem with Bud, but no matter how hard Mom tried, it was as though Bud could never accept her as his mother. When Dad was around, Bud was okay, but when Dad was away, Bud refused to do whatever Mom asked him to do. It finally reached a point, when he feared retribution from Dad and he ran away.

"I think he might be heading for your house," Dad said to Mrs. Leep. "He's been gone for almost two days."

"What am I supposed to do?" "He's your responsibility now."

Bud, however did show up at her house. She called the police and they brought him home. Mom and Dad had a long talk with him, and he never ran away again.

I was sorry for Bud. He must have felt rejection by the

one person he thought he could rely on, Mrs. Leep, the woman he initially thought of as his real mother.

Bud was not an easy kid to raise. He was full of the devil and stubborn as a mule but he never got into any serious trouble. Mostly it was stupid pranks.

There was a time I could bend both of my feet behind my head. Bud tried but he only managed to get one foot behind his head. I tried to help, and twisted the other foot until it caught behind his head.

Everything was fine until he tried to untangle his legs.

"Hey, help me. I can't get them down."

"No, you do it," I insisted.

"Mom! I'm stuck!" he screamed. "John won't help me!"

I didn't want to get in trouble so I pried his feet loose, and he never tried to do that trick again.

JOHN BRAUCHT

"CHARLES A. LINDBERGH AND ALEXIS CARREL CREATE A FORM OF ARTIFICIAL HEART FOR USE DURING CARDIAC SURGERY"

Chapter Fifteen
1936

I was 19 and Bud 16, when we decided to join the Navy. Though he was younger, he was taller and could easily pass for twenty.

We passed all the enlistment requirements but one...Bud and I had flat feet. As it turned out, it was for the best that I had not been accepted into the Navy.

Bud wanted to learn to ride Prince, but he never had much luck. The horse sensed Bud was a novice. Every time he attempted to ride him, Prince galloped back to the stable with Bud hanging on for dear life.

Actually, Prince turned out to be a well-behaved horse but when we bought him, he was a two year old and filled with spit and vinegar. One day, after his mane had been clipped, I was riding him bareback. We were heading straight down the road at a full gallop, when Prince decided to take a different route. Without any warning, he swerved to right, and with nothing to hang onto, I flew over his head into the bushes.

Fortunately, I hurt nothing more than my pride, which they say, 'goeth before a fall'. I managed to catch up with him in a friend's back yard and mounted him. I was no sooner on his back, when he took off under a closeline, and I found myself on the ground a second time. For some reason that day, he was unusually spooky, and it took some time to calm him down to the point where I was able to stay on his back.

Another time, after Bud and I harnessed Prince to the plow, he broke away and took off down the road. I called Dr. Young, the veterinarian who sold us Prince. Just as I started to tell him what happened, he looked out the window and saw Prince galloping up to his house, dragging the plow behind him.

Later, a neighbor attempted to show me how to train Prince. His method to beat the horse into obedience went against my grain so I decided to train him. I did not want anyone to break his spirit, and eventually, with kindness, love and patience, Prince became a good riding mount.

When we lived at Dixie Gardens, we had sixteen dogs. Three females had puppies about the same time. We'd always managed to find homes for them and other strays. Later on, Dad brought home a part-wolf, part German Shepherd puppy that we named Wolf.

Dovey, a toddler, who could barely walk, was playing on our front lawn. The lawn that I had recently sown with

A LIFETIME WORTH REMEMBERING

Bermuda grass was now lush and soft. I sat down and started to play with the toddler. I gave her a tiny shove and she sat down in the grass and laughed. I did this a few more times, when unexpectedly, Wolf, with a mother's protective instinct, grabbed me by the arm and growled. She had never done that before, and I never gave her a reason to do it again.

I was at work at the stone plant when I remembered that the chicken nests needed cleaning. I called Bud and asked him to burn the old straw and fill the nests with fresh straw. He grumbled at first and then agreed to the chore. He set fire to the old straw, which was too close to the chicken coop. Before he could put the fire out, smoke filled the chicken houses. When Bud raised the flaps to let the smoke escape, the fire spread to the chicken house, and the garage with the chicken batteries and the cowshed burned to the ground.

Old Mary, who was still working for us, helped Mom pull the batteries, which were on rollers, outside.

It was too late to save the chickens that died from smoke inhalation. It took Mom, myself, Old Mary, our neighbor Ruth and her brother Billy all night to salvage the broiler-sized chickens for canning. In an assembly line, we plucked the feathers and cut off the heads so they would bleed. The next day, Mom and Ruth canned the chickens in mason jars. We ate chicken for over a year and never asked Bud to light another fire.

Me, Bud, Billy and his sister used to go swimming at a small nearby lake. Bud and Billy liked to skinny dip. Billy tried every trick to get his sister to take off her clothes, but she refused and neither would I.

From time to time, I would have a crush on a few girls, but I hadn't gone steady for quite a while. I met Karen, a very sweet girl, who lived nearby. I asked her out and was overjoyed when she said, "yes". I borrowed Dad's car, and picked her up at her house. When she got in the car, she snuggled close and took me by surprise with a kiss to my cheek.

"Why did you do that?" I asked, embarrassed by her actions.

She pulled away from me with a strange look on her face.

"Because I felt like it," Susan said.

The date was nice enough, but she never went out with me again. I later realized how my question must have sounded and regretted what I had said.

The year I received the award for best drill cadet, I started going steady with Jewel Fuller. Her father worked for *Jewel Tea*, and named her after the company. Jewel and I were very compatible and before long, our romance grew more serious. I even gave her the ribbon and medal that I won for best drill cadet, which didn't make my mother too happy. I wanted to marry Jewel, but she was only sixteen, so we decided to wait another year.

David Ellis, a buddy of mine from high school, wanted to go to Hawaii and talked me into enlisting in the army. We went to the post office to enlist, but were told we would have to go to New Orleans. We were anxious to enlist, so we hitchhiked all the way.

"You're both too young to enlist," the recruiter said.

A LIFETIME WORTH REMEMBERING

"You boys are only nineteen and you have to be twenty-one to get in the service."

I was disappointed and said, "But we came all the way from Shreveport."

"I don't want to wait that long," David insisted.

The recruiter reached into his desk drawer and handed us a couple of forms. "Look," he said. "If you're that serious, take these home with you and get your parents signatures and then you can enlist."

We hitchhiked home and were dropped off by our first ride at a trucker's station. We sat at the counter and had a couple of burgers and cokes. When we finished eating, Dave went over to a trucker and asked him for a ride. I no sooner stood up to follow him, than a drunk whacked me across the face with a beer bottle. Before anyone knew what happened, the drunk ran out the door and disappeared.

I touched my lip and tasted blood.

"Oh, you poor kid," the waitress said, running over with a napkin wrapped around some ice. "Here, put this on your face."

I looked in the mirror. My lip was split open and my face swelled up like a balloon. I was grateful he didn't break my teeth.

"Where are you kids going?" the trucker said.

He must have felt sorry for me because he took us as far as Shreveport.

By the time I arrived home, most of the swelling had gone down. I told Mom and Dad what happened and they insisted I see the doctor that day. He checked my lip and decided the cut wasn't bad enough to require stitches.

After everything quieted down, I gave my parents the forms to sign.

"I think you're too young to join up," Dad said, not wanting to sign the release forms. "Why don't you learn the stone business so when I retire, I can turn it over to you."

"What about Bud? Why can't he learn the business?"

"You know he wants to stay in the academy," Mom said.

I knew she was right. Bud had begged to go to the Jefferson Military Academy in Natches, Mississippi and Dad couldn't say no to him.

"But Dad, I really want to go," I pleaded.

"I'll sign it if your mother signs it first," he said.

Mom signed the paper immediately, and then handed it to Dad.

"I just can't bring myself to do it."

After a lot of coaxing, he pushed the paper and pen in front of me. "You sign it for me."

I went over to Jewel's house to tell her that I was enlisting in the Army.

"I'm leaving to sign up in New Orleans tomorrow morning," I said.

Tears welled up in her eyes. "Please don't go, Johnny," she begged.

"I've already made up my mind, Jewel," I said. "It's a great opportunity for me."

"But what about me? I'll miss you terribly."

"I'll miss you too, but I'll be back."

"I'll wait for you, Johnny and I won't date anyone else," she sobbed, tears rolling down her cheeks.

A LIFETIME WORTH REMEMBERING

The bus pulled into New Orleans late in the evening and David and I got a room for twenty-five cents in a cheap hotel near the army recruiting station. Neither of us had much money and weren't sure when we'd be getting paid, so we filled up on a quarters worth of corn beef, cabbage and potatoes.

The next morning, we went directly to the recruiting station for our physical, and passed without any trouble. We were officially sworn in the army on July 8th, 1936.

Our first stop was Fort Benning, Georgia, and our second, Savanna, Georgia. The Sergeant marched us up to the door of a large gymnasium where we would be housed until we were ready to be shipped to Panama.

"Before we go in, I want you to take a good look at the floor inside," the Sergeant ordered.

The recruits hovered around the door to get a look. The room was set up neatly with folding cots, and the floor was waxed to a high shine.

"As you can see, those hardwood floors are beautifully maintained," the Sergeant continued, "and we expect them to remain that way until we vacate this building. So, I will tell you this and you had better remember it well. You are not to smoke or wear shoes in this room. Do I make myself clear?"

"Yes, sir," we responded.

"Good. Now get your shoes off and get inside."

It was only few days later, when a guy I didn't know sat down across from me.

"Hey, buddy," he said, handing me a lit cigarette. "Hang

onto this for a minute while I tie my shoe."

I had no sooner accepted the cigarette, than the Sergeant stepped up behind me. "Okay Braucht. You were warned. Now get yourself into the kitchen. You got KP for the week. Next time maybe you'll take me more serious when I give an order not to smoke."

It was obvious that the guy had set me up, but I realized that silence was the better part of valor, and didn't defend myself. He got up and walked away when he realized I wasn't going to squeal on him. I learned another lesson the hard way, and did not intend to take the rap for anyone again.

KP turned out to be not so bad. All I had to do was peel potatoes and prepare vegetables. I really didn't mind that much because I helped Mom around the kitchen ever since I could remember. I always believed that you could turn almost everything into something good if you tried hard enough.

A small French ship, the Chateau Thierry, came in from New York and docked at Savanna. It had been used as a cattle boat during World War I, but now it transported military troops to Panama.

I didn't get to see much of my buddy David. He was sent to Fort Clayton on the Pacific side of Panama and I was assigned to the 14th Infantry at Fort Davis, on the Atlantic side of Panama, near the Gatun Locks.

Company E was a concrete barrack three stories tall. The first floor was made up of the kitchen, offices, dining and supply rooms and a recreation area. There were no windows in the sleeping quarters on the upper floors.

A LIFETIME WORTH REMEMBERING

We were assigned one upright and one foot locker. New recruits and privates with little service time slept in the upper bunks, so it was inevitable that I would get the upper.

I had only been at Fort Davis a couple of days, when a guy in the bunk across from me said, "You had one heck of a nightmare last night."

"I did?" I asked, not remembering a thing.

"You better believe you did," he went on. "You started screaming and hollering in the middle of the night and woke me up. Then all of a sudden, you jumped at me like a bat out of you know where, but I saw you coming in time and stuck my foot in your stomach and you hit the floor."

"You're kidding," I said. It was difficult to believe that I could have done such a thing and not remember doing it.

"No, I'm not kidding. You just hit the floor and crawled back in bed and never said a word."

That was the first and only time in my life that I ever reacted like that in my sleep...to my knowledge.

We were drilled daily for six weeks at boot camp. The drill sergeants barked commands at us constantly until we got every turn and step down to perfection. I had a slight advantage over the others, having had two years of drill at the National Guard and ROTC. Winning the medal didn't hurt either. With this training in my background, I was quick to learn, and was seldom corrected.

There were a couple of towns near the Fort; Colon, which was mostly inhabited by natives and Christobal where the American and English-speaking people lived.

As soon as we completed boot camp, everyone was anxious

to have a little fun in town. The older privates decided to show the new recruits around Cologne. The first stop they headed for was the bar.

"Come on," they insisted. "We're gonna teach you rookies how to drink."

I went along. Raised a strict Baptist, and brought up by non-drinking parents, a bar was not where I wanted to be.

"I'll just have a lemonade," I said to the bartender.

He looked a little surprised at my request. The lemonade tasted a little bitter, but I didn't think too much of it. Within an hour I began to feel dizzy, and grabbed a bus back to the base.

I woke up the next morning with a terrible headache and suspected someone had spiked my drink. It was the first and last headache I have ever had of that severity.

When it came time for morning drill, several of the recruits and old-timers had hangovers, and were running into each other.

"Get those bayonets off your rifles before you kill yourselves!" the Sergeant shouted. "We don't need any stabbings during drill."

A lot of the guys spent their nights off base drinking and gambling in the poolrooms but most of their money went for prostitutes and marijuana which was called 'intelligent weed' in Panama.

In order to buy toilet articles, cigarettes or snacks at the Post Exchange, you could draw against next month's pay by buying a coupon book. You could also get a movie card for a dollar and a half that admitted you to the theater ten times, and a barber card that had to be punched. Sometimes when the men needed money fast, they would trade the book of coupons for cash, usually for about half for what they paid.

I had fifteen dollars automatically taken out of my pay each month. It was sent home for insurance and a savings account. Mom bought me a bedroom set with some of my money. *I want you to have some furniture by the time you get married*, she wrote.

Privates received twenty-one dollars a month, private first class thirty dollars, corporals forty-two dollars, and buck sergeants sixty dollars. Thirty-five cents was deducted each month to pay for the 'Sand Blast Indians' to do our kitchen duty.

I corresponded with Jewel and my parents every week. At Christmas, I sent Jewel a present, and she responded by sending me a 'Dear John' letter.

I can't wait for you any longer, John, she wrote, *and I hate to tell you this, but I'm getting married soon.*

In spite of the fact that I was very upset, I wrote and wished her the best. It was quite a surprise when I heard from her in March. She wrote, *I got a divorce, John. I realize now that you are the only man I have ever truly loved and I want to marry you.* I wrote her back immediately and said that marriage would be out of the question after what she had done. She never wrote to me again.

JOHN BRAUCHT

"LAW STUDENT CHESTER CARLSON INVENTS THE FIRST METHOD OF PHOTOCOPYING-XEROGRAPHY"

Chapter Sixteen
1937

It wasn't long before I was promoted to Private First Class. When you made High Expert Rifleman, you were given a five-dollar raise. We spent a lot of time on the rifle range and no one was exempt from practice. We used a 30 caliber Spring Field bolt action that was loaded by pushing the shells into the rifle from a five-clip holder. We had to qualify on the 200, 300 and 500 yard range, using slow and rapid fire.

There was a right and left fishtail wind on the day we were qualifying for the 500-yard range. This made it almost impossible to hit the target since the wind kept changing direction. I lost a couple of points before I realized the situation and waited until the wind was directly behind me before firing. My shots were dead on target. I made High Expert Rifleman, and got my five-dollar raise.

After the 500, came the toughie... the 1000 yard. We were allowed to use a scope on our rifle with a larger bull's eye target to hit. Each squad had only one automatic rifle that could be assigned to anyone at anytime. There were four companies in a battalion and the fourth company of each battalion used machine guns. Each company trained only those men who were well qualified with rifles to use the machine gun.

We learned to take each weapon apart and clean and reassemble it, either in the dark or blindfolded.

After weapon training, we could volunteer for special sports competition. I always loved track and field, and immediately leapt at the chance to participate. I swam, ran long distance, pole-vaulted, and ran the high and low hurdle.

We were getting ready to have a tug-of-war, and I recalled the time when we held a 'boy against girl' tug-of-war at church. I told the girls, "Stand sideways, dig in your heels, keep your bodies straight and grab the rope with your hands close together." When they assumed the position, I continued, "Now take a short step back on your right leg, give the rope a jerk and let go!"

This technique succeeded in catching the boys off guard, and gave the girls the advantage they needed to win.

I was determined to implement this strategy. Each finalist team tied a rope around the waist of the biggest and strongest guy they could find. We were equally matched, but I had our group try the jerk and release and our team won the competition.

At the time we were stationed in Panama, Gatun Lake was considered one of the largest man-made lakes in the world. For fun we'd swim out to the privately owned boats, and discovered that one large beautiful sailboat was owned by the famous movie star, Errol Flynn.

I loved swimming and took a lifeguard course at the local YMCA. As a result, I was given the job of lifeguard at the base pool. Commissioned officers and their families swam in the morning and enlisted men in the p.m. An incident occurred when a young attractive woman climbed out of the pool. Her wet bathing suit clung to her shapely body and there was more of her revealed when she was wet than when she was dry.

Soon the word got out about the woman and her sexy bathing suit. The enlisted men started showing up early in the morning just to see the woman climb out of the pool. Before long, the pool was filled with enlisted men. Eventually, there was a notice banning enlisted men from arriving at the pool before one p.m.

While we were on the Panama side of the locks, I learned to ride the waves on the shores of the Caribbean Sea. This was a wonderful experience as most of the guys, like myself were from the mid west, and had never stepped foot in an ocean.

During this period, the men slept a lot in the afternoon. At four o'clock, they were awakened. Each squad was expected to clean the barracks, sidewalks, porch and latrine.

The men on special duty were exempt, and allowed to sleep during this time, as they worked different shifts. I was assigned a bunk in an acting corporal's area. Apparently no one was notified that I had special duty and was not to be disturbed.

When I was awakened at four o'clock, I explained that I

had special assignment and didn't have to get up and went back to sleep. I was awakened a third time and did something I had never done before or since. I raced after the guy and caught up with him on the porch.

"If you don't leave me alone," I yelled, shaking my fist in his face. "I'm going to knock you over this railing!" With that, I shoved him away, and went back to bed.

The next day, Charge of Quarters notified me that Captain Douglas wanted to see me immediately. I reported to his office on the double.

"Private Braucht, reporting as ordered, Sir," I said, giving him a sharp salute.

"At ease, Private," Captain Douglas responded.

I relaxed, wondering what was so important.

He looked me squarely in the eye. "When a man who outranks you and gives you an order, you are to obey that order. Then if you feel it is out of order, report it to the first sergeant. Do you understand, Braucht?"

"Yes, sir," I said, with another salute.

"Good. Then we understand each other. You're dismissed."

With another salute, and an about face, I left his office. Later, I was surprised to be promoted to corporal. What I didn't understand was...why I got the promotion and the guy who woke me up didn't. But I didn't care, as I also received a raise in pay, which meant I was now earning forty-seven dollars a month; forty-two dollars as a corporal and five dollars as an Expert Rifleman.

That promotion led to my being assigned to 'Special Task' with a Colonel. He advised me that his men would be trained in various fields and my responsibility was to see that the men were expert with the rifle.

There was a rumor going around that all non-citizens in the military would be discharged and lose all benefits. One of the cooks in the outfit, who was from Portugal, had never obtained his citizenship. Married with several children, he grew very depressed thinking that his family would lose all benefits if he were discharged. So, one night, he put a rifle under his chin and pulled the trigger. I heard it was a horrible sight, as part of his head stuck to the ceiling. However, he was given an honorable funeral, with all platoons in attendance, and I was happy to hear that his family received full benefits. I was a member of the squad that fired a salute in his honor.

After the men became expert with the rifle, the next assignment was normal and jungle combat training. The use of hand and arm signals was of utmost importance when silence was necessary. These silent signals could not be detected to give away our strategy or location.

Targets were arranged to appear and disappear, and each man knew which target was his. Working as a two-man team, a man carried half a pup tent to set up camp. We also carried water, food, extra clothes, mosquito netting, blankets, machetes and first aid kits that contained iodine to purify water. Real ammunition was used for targets and blanks for practice.

Survival tactics taught us how to remove the thick husks from coconuts, and the best times to use them for the milk and meat. There were animals and an abundance of fruit and vegetables to eat but we learned to distinguish between which were edible and which were poisonous.

The natives made charcoal by setting fire to a pile of wood and covering it with dirt. At the right time, the wood would be uncovered and set aside to be used like coal, as my grandparents did when I was a boy.

In the pitch darkness, we stumbled across treacherous rocky ground, strewn with stumps and straggling roots, along a high escarpment. One false move meant a fall into the water below, so we could warn the man behind us about any obstacle in the path.

We found chunks of phosphorus and attached them on the pack of the man in front of us. The phosphorus acted like a reflector on the back of a bicycle and helped us to stay together in the dark.

Deeper into the jungle, we reached a shallow swamp and were ordered to make bivouac there. We cut tree limbs shaped like a Y, which were used as stakes and driven into the ground. Long branches were laid across the stakes to form a platform, which we then covered with moss, leaves and grass.

It didn't take us long to realize that the moss and leaves were loaded with mites. After a miserable night of scratching and no sleep, we smartened up and only used grass after that.

We no sooner broke camp, when the early morning sun broke through. By now we were starving and looked forward to our K Ration breakfast of corned beef Willie that looked more like dog food.

K Rations improved during the Korean War since everything you could possibly want was packed in cans.

A LIFETIME WORTH REMEMBERING

On another jungle maneuver, I must not have tucked the mosquito netting completely under my blankets. I scratched throughout the night and was covered with mosquito bites when I got up in the morning. I landed in the infirmary only to awaken three days later and learn I had yellow fever.

Even though the United States government made every effort to control the mosquitoes in the Canal Zone of Panama, there was no attempt to control them in the jungles. I was fortunate that I didn't catch anything else while I was there.

All units except for maintenance and guard patrol were transferred from the Atlantic to the Pacific. This feat had never been accomplished before. You really couldn't say from east to west because the entrance side of the Atlantic is actually west of the Pacific. There was no road from one coast to the other, only railroad tracks.

Each unit took turns clearing a way through the dense jungle using bolos and machetes. Our uniform for the excursion, were leggings, an undershirt, a long sleeve olive green woolen shirt, a lightweight pith helmet, and denim pants. We perspired a lot in the humid heat, and our loose outer clothing acted as a cooling system.

New latrines were dug each day. Logs were used for 'seats' and canvas draped for privacy. Pack mules carried extra rations. At night, one unit was moved forward to practice combat while other units attempted to infiltrate the lines.

By the time we reached the Chagres River, three mules carrying heavy loads lost their footing in the swift current and drowned.

As we approached a large clearing on the Pacific side,

we came upon the Army and Navy receiving and transmitting towers, which were the tallest towers than I had ever seen.

A kitchen crew was waiting for our arrival with fresh coffee and bread. I never drank coffee before, but after being up all night, tired, hungry and thirsty, I was grateful for anything. With a lot of milk and sugar in a little coffee, it tasted pretty good.

After a short rest, we headed toward Costa Rica to Madang Dam, where we had lunch. Our next stop was the Chorrera Falls. We spent a few days there, fascinated by the chattering Spider monkeys swinging from tree to tree and sloths. These slow moving creatures hung onto the trees with their powerful claws, eating until they were full. Then they would let go, fall to the ground, and just lie there.

We cooled off by diving from the top of the falls to the pool below.

One of the men was resting on the ground with his hat over his head. He was unaware that a coral snake had crawled over him and was coiled around his hat. Careful not to startle the man or the snake, I held my breath and watched while the snake crawled to the ground. I reached for my machete and with one swift slice, cut off the snake's head. The guy didn't even wake up. I skinned the snake, wrapped the skin around a bamboo shoot, and kept it for a souvenir.

After completing our jungle combat training, we were shipped back to the base in cattle cars, where we were met by a band. Dirty and exhausted, after being in the jungle for weeks, it was rejuvenating and touching to be greeted so warmly. It lifted our spirits and our morale. As we stepped off the train with our chests and chins held high, our spirits and morals lifted, we marched in like fresh troops.

The main goals of our regiment were to prepare for defense combat and to guard the Gatun Locks. By now, we were experienced to guard the perimeter of the fort as well as the locks.

The companies sent a designated number of troops for guard duty and every man was meticulously inspected. The best-dressed troops in body and equipment appearance were chosen to be the base commander's aide for that day. The men spent a lot of time and money to have their uniforms specially tailored and pressed and some went as far as to wear expensive *Stetson* hats. Shoes were shined with jeweler's rouge and rifle stocks buffed like fine furniture. To be qualified for guard duty all orders had to be memorized.

One such order was to walk the post in a military manner, keep alert, observe everything in sight and within hearing, and allow no one to pass without proper authority.

Most posts on the base were considered 'walking posts', but I was assigned to the towers where I observed the boats passing through the locks. While on duty at the Panama Canal, which is considered a modern marvel, I was fortunate to see the canal in full operation. I watched in fascination as huge metal doors closed allowing the water in until a boat was high enough to enter the next level.

When it finally reached the Gatun Lake level, it then entered into the Pacific side of the canal, where it would be lowered to the Pacific Ocean level. Boats going through from Pacific to Atlantic reversed the procedure. The Pacific was higher than the Atlantic.

Guard duty lasted two hours on and four off, but you were expected to remain in the guardhouse during off time, in the event of an emergency. U.S. troops were stationed there in the event a major defense was necessary.

'Fatigue Duty' took up a lot of time when we were not doing more important activities. One time after we had cut through grass and brush with bolo knifes on the mortar range, the noncom in charge would tell jokes. Some were very offensive, but no one was in a position to object. I was brought up in a family that never told dirty stories.

One weekend, I decided to go to a restaurant considered to be the best in town. It was crowded, and I spotted two sailors sitting at a large table and asked if I might join them. They smiled pleasantly, and nodded for me to take a seat. They were German and spoke very little English.

Speaking no German, I tried a few words in Spanish, and was pleased to find that they understood. It seemed we had all studied Spanish in high school. As a result of our conversation, they invited me to visit their pocket battleship, *The Dutchland.*

I took them up on their invitation, and was given a tour with a detailed explanation of the entire ship's operation, including the weapons it was carrying.

At lunch, one of the sailors brought up the subject of their dictator. "Adolph Hitler," he said, "is like your Roosevelt."

"In what way," I asked, seeing no resemblance between the two.

"I mean, Hitler has much power, as does your president,"

A LIFETIME WORTH REMEMBERING

he said with a smile. "They are both very charismatic and powerful men."

We spent a few more days together, getting to know each other better, until one day they told me they were ready to ship out. I later learned that their sister ship, *The Graf Spee* was sunk off the coast of Argentina during the war. I have often thought of those fine young men, who were fighting for their country just as I was fighting for mine, and wondered if they survived the war.

During the two years I spent in Panama, the National Lottery was going strong. It was common knowledge that the majority of the people who spent the most and lost the most money, unfortunately were the poor, the ones who could least afford to lose. Making matters worse, the money spent on the National Lottery also took money out of circulation. This caused an increase in crime and a decrease in the filing of tax returns. The Lottery ended up adversely effecting the Panamanian educational system and business, and a rumor persisted that the entire operation was corrupt.

Mr. Brazil, the base photographer and his wife developed the snap shots we took. They were excellent at their job and photographed everything of interest on the base, in the jungle and the locks. I was able to acquire photographs of President Roosevelt's trip through the canal that he took the previous year.

In addition to their photography business, they also operated a small sightseeing boat. One day, a group of us took the boat down the coast to Portobelo. We were walking along the shore, when Mrs. Brazil stopped and pointed out several human skulls lying in the sand. She picked one up in each hand and her husband snapped her picture standing in front of a tall monument. We continued on to an old graveyard with markers dating back to the early fifteen hundreds.

A nearby fort was in fairly good shape. It consisted of a large central building with two arched doorways and several rectangular ones. Cannons lay on the ground behind the still standing walls. A statue of *The Black Christ* at the church was displayed on a mobile platform for the annual religious celebration.

I took another interesting excursion to the Sand Blast Islands on a larger boat. (The mainland is called Cordillera De San Blas.) Permission had to be obtained to visit the largest island and no one was allowed to stay overnight on any island.

The natives, who traveled from island to island in canoes, developed large muscular chests and arms, but their legs from less exercise, were thin by comparison. They earned money by selling parakeets and indigenous souvenirs. We couldn't buy the birds, because pets were not allowed on the base.

One of my souvenir purchases was a woman's peasant blouse. With it came a delightful native custom.

When a female child is born, her mother begins preparing a *trousseau* for her wedding. The mother cuts out patterns in various shapes and materials, then the delicate pieces are over-laid, and hand sewn on the blouses, forming intricate and beautiful designs.

On the day of the girl's wedding, the ritual begins. The bride is buried waist deep in the sand, while family and friends throw water on her. The blouses, which the girl has not seen before, are strung on a rope for all to see and admire for the first time. Her long hair is cut short, the sign that she is now a married woman.

Young girls and women proudly wore gold rings in their noses. If they are too poor to purchase a ring, they cover their noses in shame. Although female children wore clothing, young boys wore nothing, or at most, a shirt.

The Community Church in Christobal had a wonderful choir that I enjoyed listening to. On Sunday mornings, the choir sang in the loft, but sat with the congregation at night. One Sunday evening, after the service was over, a gentleman introduced himself as the choir director, and requested that I join his group. I informed him that I had never sung in a choir, nor could I read music, or in fact, carry a tune. He smiled, insisting that it didn't make any difference, and encouraged me to join the choir.

I had always been able to imitate most sounds, especially if I stood beside someone who could sing tenor or bass. With enough practice, I was able to sing rather well. I preferred bass as it came easier for me, but was later told by an opera teacher that I had a tenor's voice.

When my term of enlistment drew near, I was given a choice to return home by way of either the East or West Coast. I chose the West Coast but there was a delay. It was fortunate delay, for I ended up sailing on the Republic, which was a larger and better ship in every way.

It was September and the weather was cool when we

arrived at Angel Island. We took the ferry into town, by way of Alcatraz and had enough time to see the sights in San Francisco and Oakland where I picked up a few souvenirs.

"USING STAINLESS STEEL, ENGLISH SURGEON PHILIP WILES PERFORMS THE FIRST TOTAL ARTIFICIAL HIP REPLACEMENT"

Chapter Seventeen
1938

My next stop was home. At last I was back in Shreveport, Louisiana, where my parents welcomed me at the train with open arms and good news. They just finished building a new home in the south section of Broadmore near the church.

However, I was saddened to learn that Dad was not well. All the years of hard work, and the lingering effects he suffered in World War I, were taking its toll. The doctor advised him to eat a can of spinach a day and to do a lot of running and walking and Dad took his advice. It must have been sound advice, as he lived to the ripe old age of ninety-six.

I was only home for a few days, when my old girlfriend Jewel and her mother came to see me. Given the circumstances of what had happened in the past, it was an uncomfortable visit and somewhat strained as no one mentioned anything regarding our former relationship. I was relieved, as I no longer wanted to date Jewel.

JOHN BRAUCHT

I went to work for my father, and was given a new position of selling granite and marble monuments on the road. I immediately purchased a two-year-old grey Chevrolet, in mint condition for $250.00. My territory covered northern Louisiana. I was paid by commission, and apparently did an excellent job as Dad said I made him more money than any other salesman who ever worked for him did.

Many times I was asked to preach on Sunday at different churches when I was away selling the monuments, with an open invitation to stay at the homes of the church members.

The regular Sunday school teacher was going to be absent one Sunday. "Would you take over my class for me, John," he asked.

"Of course," I said, happy to have the opportunity to teach the Bible.

I told the boys about the disciple Paul, who wrote thirteen books of the New Testament and how he supported himself by making tents.

That night, I asked God to be like Paul. I told Him I wanted to preach the Bible and support myself like Paul did in the Scriptures.

It would be many years before God would answer my request but not in the way I intended.

When I wasn't away selling monuments, Albert Scaparelli, an old school buddy and I, decided to go into business making and selling doormats. He bought some machinery that stripped old automobile tires, punched holes, threaded wire through the holes and clamped them secure. His job was to make the mats. My job was to sell them door-to-door and to hardware stores.

Then times got hard and doormats, which were considered a luxury item, stopped selling so I found work at Hemingway and Johnson's Furniture and Appliance Store. Sometimes I worked in the store and sometimes sold door-to-door.

I had a couple of ideas that I thought would make outside sales more profitable. I followed ice trucks and after they made a delivery at a house, I would talk to the homeowner and convince them that it would be more economical if they owned their own refrigerator. It could be bought for about the same monthly cost of the ice, less the inconvenience of icemen trudging through their house. Plus they could make their own ice and their food would keep better and longer. I also followed laundry vans, and used the same approach when I spoke about the benefits of owning their own washing machine.

My outside sales increased, and I was paid more commission on merchandise sold in the homes.

During the depression, the Broadmore Church could not meet some of their financial obligations. Dad either made the payments himself, or raised the money for the church by selling some of their property. He had his attorney take care of all the legal transactions, at no expense to the church.

The church stated that it might not have lasted, if Dad had not given so much of himself. The Broadmore Baptist Church gives a true picture of Dad's contributions and his unselfish work in the Fiftieth Anniversary Journal, published by their church. They wrote that if it wasn't for his dedication, the church might not have survived.

JOHN BRAUCHT

Dad was the most honest and fair man I have ever known. Builders sought him out, handed him blue prints and gave him the job...on his reputation and the fact that all the stone work in the area was done by him. He helped many people during those years, by giving them work at the plant even if he didn't need the help.

"GERMAN AND SOVIET ARMED FORCES OCCUPY POLAND, BEGINNING WORLD WAR II"

Chapter Eighteen
1939

It wasn't long before the National Guard called me for a special camp tour. The growing Hitler movement in Germany brought this about.

I took a correspondence course for Second Lieutenant in the reserves. After successfully completing it, the National Guard in Shreveport was changed to the 204th Coast Artillery. I was now required to take additional courses to qualify as an officer in that particular unit. With the tests behind me, I then reported to the County Court House to take an oral examination by the Army Reserve Board. Everything went well and I was promoted to Second Lieutenant.

While I was in Panama, my parents moved their membership back to Highland. They had also selected Harriet Herrin, who was active in the church to be my bride. The problem was I had no idea of their intentions.

"We've invited Harriet over for Sunday dinner," Dad

informed me one evening.

"How come?" I asked.

"Oh, your mother and I thought you two would enjoy each others company. That's all."

"But I see her at church all the time," I said, making it sound like a protest. "And we really don't have a lot in common."

"Well, we think you ought to get to know Harriet better," Dad said. "She's a very lovely girl, John."

I knew there was an ulterior motive. He had been telling me what a nice girl Harriet was for several weeks. She was nice enough, but I considered her just a good friend. It was no use arguing with Dad. When he made up his mind, it was set.

Harriet arrived the following Sunday. She looked rather pretty, and brought a small bouquet of flowers for Mom as a house gift. We engaged in a pleasant conversation during dinner and after we had eaten, Dad stood up and yawned.

"We're going to take a nap now," he said. "We know you two kids want to be alone."

I gave Mom a beseeching look, but she only shrugged and followed Dad out of the room.

Now the conversation with Harriet felt strained. Even though I liked her, I was not interested in her as a girlfriend and definitely had no intentions to marry her. We sat around for the rest of the evening and talked small talk. The conversation ended with my making a decision to join the choir at Highland Church.

Mr. Stroup, the choir director was surprised to learn that I had sung with the Panamanian choir, and welcomed

A LIFETIME WORTH REMEMBERING

me to the group.

While in the midst of practice one evening, Mr. Stroup tapped his baton against his music stand.

"May I have your attention, please," he said. "Someone is singing off key. I must say that I have been guilty of that myself at times." He smiled and pointed to a young lady in the front row. "But Miss Luella Dutt is never off key."

She smiled back, and I had never seen a more beautiful smile in my life. It was that very smile that eventually captivated my heart.

Rehearsal over, I mustered enough courage to follow her out into the hall. She went into the pastor's office, where she was employed as his secretary, and I stood in front of the doorway, waiting for her to come out. Finally the door opened and I said, "Hello Miss Dutt. My name is John Braucht and I was wondering if you would you care to go to the fair with me this weekend?"

Her first response was one of surprise. "Oh," she said. Then she relaxed and smiled her beautiful smile again. "I'll ask my mother and let you know. And by the way John, you can call me Lue."

I presumed that she was leery of going out with a soldier because soldiers did not have a very good reputation with women.

I couldn't wait for the next choir rehearsal. I was the first one there and when Lue came in, I hurried over and sat next to her.

"Did you ask your mother?" I blurted out.

"Yes," she said, with that beautiful smile. "My mother said it was okay for me to go out with you. And she told us to have a good time."

I breathed a sigh of relief. "That's great."

"Did you know that our parents know each other, John?"

"No, I didn't. What did they say about me?"

"They said you are a very nice boy." She modestly lowered her head and continued, "But I didn't need them to tell me that."

Lue and I had a wonderful first date at the Shreveport State Fair. We had a lot in common. She came from a good family, and we belonged to the same religion. She wanted to travel someday and I certainly did. She was kind and gentle, liked animals and children, and even admitted she liked to cook. We were like a couple of kids that day. We went on all the amusements and especially enjoyed the caterpillar ride. We played a game requiring us to put a dime on a particular color, which represented the same color on a spinning wheel. We got fortunate and won a couple of dollars. It was the first time either one of us had ever gambled, and the last time.

"You shouldn't have spent so much money, John," Lue said as we were walking home. "It was so extravagant."

"It was only five dollars," I said, thinking nothing was too extravagant for her.

By the time we got to her house I made a decision and said, "We're going to get married, Lue."

She looked surprised and laughed. "You must be crazy."

But I was serious and it wasn't long before I stopped by the church to see Lue after choir practice. "Would you please come outside. I have something to show you."

A LIFETIME WORTH REMEMBERING

She followed me back to the car, and I reached in the front seat for a measuring tape. "Here," I said, "let me see your left hand."

She held out her hand. "What are you doing, John?"

"I want to measure your finger. I want to make sure the ring I get you is the right size."

She looked surprised. "What kind of ring is that?"

"I guess you'd call it an engagement ring."

The next time I saw her, I took a diamond ring out of my pocket, got down on my knee and slipped it on her finger. My heart was pounding as I asked, "Will you be my wife?"

"Yes, I will," she said without hesitation.

"Now it's official," I said. "We're engaged. All we have to do now is set a date."

When I told my parents that I proposed to Lue that afternoon, Dad asked, "What's wrong with Harriet?"

"I don't love her, that's what's wrong," I said. "I love Lue Dutt and we're getting married."

Mom stared at Dad. "Well, if John loves Lue, then we're just going to have to love her too. Right Glenn?"

Dad grinned. "You're always right, my love."

Lue's mother bought her a cedar chest that Lue nicknamed IWW. It stood for 'I Wonder When?' and meant, 'I wonder when I'm going to get married'. Mrs. Caylor, the preacher's wife gave her a shower and a six-piece setting of Fastora Crystal and her friends completed the set. Lue's mother made her wedding gown and the bridesmaid's dresses.

The Highland Church overflowed with friends and family

on the day of our wedding. Bud, was my best man, was so nervous that I almost pulled him to the altar.

After a wonderful reception, Lue and I left to begin our honeymoon. We bought bus tickets for Monterrey, Mexico but stopped off first to visit my brother Owen, his wife Joyce and my cousin Dale. After continuing on to Laredo, and Nuevo Laredo, we decided to forego Monterrey and save some of the $100.00 my Dad gave us for a wedding present.

After the honeymoon we rented an upstairs apartment next to Lue's mother. I was now employed for Dad as an Assistant Draftsman and earned $20.00 a week. Lue continued working for Pastor Caylor at the church, and made $8.00 a week. By budgeting our money carefully, we were able to tithe and still have a little left over to put into a savings account.

"THE FIRST COLOR TELEVISION BROADCAST AIRS, USING SYSTEM DEVELOPED BY PETER CARL GOLDMARK"

Chapter Nineteen
1940

I decided to take a job with the Life and Casualty Insurance Company, and my starting pay was $35.00 a week. I did extremely well in the debit department, and in just a few months I was making $75.00 a week. The most difficult part of the job was locating the houses in the country, since most roads in those days were not named, and houses not numbered. Sometimes, when I made my collections, the insured did not have enough money to pay for their premium, so we bartered. I'd accept a chicken and in turn would pay their premium.

Our first investment was a house we purchased for $3,800.00 with just a few hundred dollars down. We rented it out for a small profit and sold it in a couple of years for $7,600.00.

JOHN BRAUCHT

"THE JAPANESE ATTACK U.S. ARMED FORCES AT PEARL HARBOR ON DECEMBER 7, 1941"

Chapter Twenty
1941

It was on January 6th, my 24th birthday, when I reported to the National Guard at Palacios, Texas. Most of the married men were there without their families, and I was no exception.

I joined a Baptist church, and was given a warm reception by the congregation. Mrs. Harbison and her young daughter Lois invited Billy, a friend from back home and myself to their house for dinner and a game of dominos. This so-called friend had different ideas about the visit than I did. He decided I was a threat to his social life and told my brother Bud that I had eyes for Lois.

Bud was a private in the army at the same base and chose to pass this information on to my wife. Although Lue did not believe the lie, she and Bud's wife, Marjorie came to Palacios to spend Easter Sunday with us.

JOHN BRAUCHT

I was sent to Galveston, Texas to learn the use of the M-3 Director, a computerized instrument that determines when and where to fire anti-aircraft cannons. These instruments would be used in the United States in the event of an enemy attack, and shipped overseas to be used in any war zone.

When I had time off, I was able to do a little bartering on the side. I raised Jersey White Giant chickens and traded them to a restaurant owner in exchange for free meals.

I was appointed secretary to take minutes on a court martial board.

A drunken enlisted man had been riding on the fender of a car. The car hit a raised culvert in the road, and the man was thrown off the car and run over by the rear wheel. He was found guilty, and discharged without benefits.

We didn't have a typist, so I volunteered Lue to do the typing.

When the training at Galveston was completed, we returned to Mrs. Harbison's house in Palacios. I had a few days off and was able to spend them with Lue. It was in the spring and we spent the time picnicking in the country where beautiful wild flowers, especially blue bonnets were coming into bloom.

I wanted to get ahead in the service and decided to apply for pilot training. I was sent to Victoria, Texas for an extensive physical, where I was put through every imaginable test. I passed with 'flying' colors but, because I was not a college graduate, I could only be accepted if I took a college equivalent test.

A LIFETIME WORTH REMEMBERING

I took the test and passed it only to discover that I was now in the precarious position of losing my commission if I washed out during cadet training. I changed my mind about taking the cadet training and returned to camp.

I was the Officer of the Day when Japan bombed Pearl Harbor. I heard the news over the radio and was stunned.

Roosevelt described the sneak attack as 'a day of infamy'. The nation was in shock and war declared. Our unit was ordered to California to be shipped to the Philippines. I loaded my crying wife into our *Plymouth*, and sent her back to the apartment in Shreveport.

As I was about to board the train in Houston, Colonel McBride tapped me on the shoulder.

"You won't be going, Braucht," he said. "Orders just came in and you're being sent to pilot training."

"Sir," I replied. "I don't want to give up my commission and go through all that hazing again."

"You don't have to son. You can go through training with no chance of losing your commission." He smiled. "And your wife can go with you and you can live off base."

"Thank you, Sir," I said with a sharp salute. I was relieved and excited. Now I'd be able to become a pilot, and further my education at the same time. This would ensure a substantial raise in my pay. I couldn't wait to share the good news with my wife.

The new orders sent me to Pine Bluff, Arkansas, where Lue and I were able to find lodging with a kind family living near the base. They gave us their teen-age son's room, and later were saddened to learn that he lost his life in combat as a navy pilot.

Classes began at a civilian field with college level civilian instructors. My first aircraft experience was in a low wing *Fairchild* open cockpit. We learned to fly literally by 'the seat of our pants'.

Mister Hatfield, the instructor, was in the front seat of the tandem and I was in the rear. On our first flight he instructed me to remove my feet from rudder controls while he turned the aircraft upside down. I was then expected to get my feet back on the controls, which at first I was unable to do. What I did do though was to get airsick for the first week, and use up all the airsick bags.

I attended morning classes to learn about aircraft maintenance and navigation etc. Now, with more education and experience under my belt, I was relieved that I didn't have any trouble on my solo flight because Hatfield taught me in a calm and reassuring voice. With Hatfield in charge, we were given designated points to fly over and then return to home base.

It was my last day of training, and we were heading back to home base, when Hatfield said, "Okay, John. We got some time to kill, so lets practice shooting some emergency landings."

I was quite familiar with what we called 'strangefield landings', and was grateful to get all the experience I could.

"Okay, let's go," I said, giving him a thumbs up.

He cut the engine and I was on my own.

We were flying fairly low over open countryside. I looked for a safe place to land and didn't see a large enough spot to bring the plane down safely. I circled the area again

A LIFETIME WORTH REMEMBERING

for a better look and spotted an open field. It was none too soon as we were losing altitude fast, so I let the plane glide in the direction of the field.

We weren't allowed to actually land on private property. The intent was to fly close to the ground without making contact.

The ground was only a few feet away before I hit the throttle and began the climb back up.

"Very good, John!" Hatfield yelled from the rear, "For a beginner! But let's try it again, and this time, mow the grass."

I laughed, and repeated the procedure until I was able to do it with ease.

Toward the end of the flight, he asked, "Are you up to trying a few acrobatics?"

I wasn't sure that I wanted him to know that I still got airsick but I managed to say, "Yes."

"Okay then, John. Finish with a couple of snap roles."

I snapped the plane upside down and immediately snapped back in the opposite direction. Just I feared, my dinner ended up in the bag.

When we landed, Hatfield jumped out of the plane and said, "Did I see what I think I saw?"

I knew exactly what he meant and exactly what he saw. "Yes sir," I said. "You saw the bag."

"How long has this been going on?" he asked.

"Since we started acrobatics," I answered, still feeling the effects of nausea.

He scratched his head and looked at me in amazement. "If I had known this earlier, I would have disqualified you.

JOHN BRAUCHT

But if you fly as well as you did and can fill a bag at the same time and toss it overboard, you're okay with me." He held out his hand. "And I'll be glad to recommend you highly."
 Fortunately, I never had any trouble flying in larger aircraft and eventually outgrew being sick in smaller planes.
 My next flight training assignment was at Randolph Air Force Base. Lue and I packed up our belongings and took off for San Antonio, Texas in our little Plymouth and found a small apartment near the base. My brother Owen and his wife, Joyce were also living in San Antonio, and Lue and I visited them often. Owen later became a tail gunner in a B-17 and lost several of his toes when his feet froze during a combat flight.

Lieutenant Synder, the instructor at Randolph was nothing like Hatfield. He yelled and complained and nothing ever satisfied him. He scheduled me for a washout with his commander, Captain Duncan. After the flight was completed, Duncan told Snyder, "I can't find anything wrong with Braucht's performance. So what seems to be the problem?"
 "He just doesn't cut it," was Synder's only response.
 Later that day, Duncan called me into his office and said. "What's the deal with you and Synder?"
 "I don't know, sir," I said honestly. "Everything I do seems to infuriate him."
 "I gather that by talking to him. Anything else you might be able to tell me?"
 I didn't want to get anyone in trouble, but my career was at stake. "Well, sir," I said. "Lieutenant Snyder gave me orders to do specific maneuvers that he was fully aware I

had no previous training in."

"In that case, then, I think I need to look into this matter," Duncan said.

"Thank you, sir," I said, starting to leave.

"Just a Moment, Braucht."

I turned to face him. "Yes, sir?"

Duncan smiled at me. "I think you ought to know that I considered your performance outstanding."

"Thank you sir," I said. "I really appreciate your telling me that."

I later learned that Duncan checked Synder's records and discovered that Synder washed out every officer who had ever flown with him. It turned out that he was angry that he went through hazing and the student officers had not, so he took out his resentment on the officers by washing them out. It came as no disappointment to anyone when another instructor replaced Synder.

While we were learning to fly formation, we would gently tap the formation plane's wing with our plane's wing. This was really against the rules but we were young pilots spreading our wild oats in the air.

We were also trained in the basics of night flying. We were quite anxious about flying in the dark, but with the expert help of our instructors, we became proficient at day and night flying.

The third and last pilot training was at Hinsley Field, in Houston. Our instructor was not only a captain in the Air Force, but a licensed physician who chose to instruct pilots rather than to practice medicine.

"Any flight you guys can walk away from is a good flight," the captain said with a grin. "But remember, too much caution can be dangerous. The point I want to make is, you must learn to make well thought out and careful decisions, and then act quickly. You're lives will depend on it. My mother used to say," the captain continued, "'son, fly low and slow'."

We trained in a twin engine *Beach*, initially flying with the captain. Then I'd pilot the plane with another student pilot acting as co-pilot. Before take-off, the co-pilots job was to go over the checklist, and the pilot's job was to check each step to make sure everything was in working order.

An incident occurred when I was acting as co-pilot that could have been disastrous. After I read the checklists, we pulled out on the runway, and I noticed the pilot starting on a second checklist. This was both unnecessary and dangerous. Other planes were due to land, and the runway had to be cleared.

"What are you doing?" I demanded to know.

"I'm checking the check list again," the pilot answered.

"Are you crazy!" I said, grabbing the checklist out of his hands. "We've got to take off now before someone lands on top of us!"

We learned to fly completely on instruments. A small machine called a link trainer that looked like an airplane was used. It was dark inside except for the light of our instruments. Later in our airplane we were in what we called a hood and were required to fly the aircraft only by the instruments and gauges on our panel, which were very

A LIFETIME WORTH REMEMBERING

crude and depended on our being able to calculate seconds accurately.

At the end of our training, we were given an identification card with our photo, description, qualifications and seal of approval. Graduation from pilot's school was a big event. It meant a ceremony, parade and the presentation of wings. My wife and parents were there to help celebrate the occasion. Unfortunately it turned out to be a rather embarrassing one for me. Normally the new pilots were expected to pin their wings on their wives or girlfriends...I pinned them on my mother instead.

JOHN BRAUCHT

A LIFETIME WORTH REMEMBERING

"THE MOST POPULAR SONG IS IRVING BERLIN'S 'WHITE CHRISTMAS'"

Chapter Twenty-One
1942

After receiving my wings, the next assignment was at Key Field in Meridian, Mississippi. As usual, housing was not plentiful but Lue and I managed to find a roomy attic apartment and later a house.

The squadron commander at Key Field was a West Point man. He checked us out in an A-20, a light two-engine bomber, which was the same make of plane I had flown before. I was to lie on my stomach behind the cockpit along with two other pilots until we learned to operate all the switches blindfolded.

Next, we practiced flying low, just feet off the ground. Sometimes when we buzzed over fields, the terrified farmers flattened themselves to the ground, and probably cursed us.

After successfully completing this training, I had a couple of days off which I spent helping Lue finish decorating the Meridian apartment.

"Everything is looking real nice, John," she said.

"So I guess it's time for another move." And she was always right.

The new orders took us to Alexandria, Louisiana. We no sooner arrived than I went to see the Adjutant.

"I need the afternoon off to find a place to live," I said.

He laughed.

"What's so funny?" I said.

"You're leaving for England, so I wouldn't bother renting a place yet."

I sat down, and sighed. "My poor wife. Just when she thought we'd be able to settle down."

"Well, maybe the next time Braucht, but for now, you're going to be catching a boat out of Camp Hawn, New Jersey tomorrow evening."

Lue returned to Shreveport and moved in with her mother. Most of my uniforms and Lue's clothing were packed in a large steamer trunk and was shipped to Alexandria. Because of my sudden departure to England, they did not arrive in time for me to take them with me. The military would not forward the trunk because of limited space and shipped it to Lue in Shreveport. Lue mailed my uniforms to Lambourn Downs in Berkshire County where I would be stationed.

Our squadron sailed to England on a Dutch liner, which was quite luxurious, compared to the Panama boat trips. We were five to a cabin, two officers from Kentucky, two black pilots and myself. The officers had no intentions of sharing a room with blacks. They requested to be reassigned better quarters and were given a smaller room instead.

A LIFETIME WORTH REMEMBERING

One evening, while I was out on deck, I struck up a conversation with one of the black pilots. He was very intelligent and personable. I thought it a shame that the officers judged a man because of the color of his skin and not the caliber of the man himself. The replacement officers were not biased, and we all got along for the duration of the trip.

One of my roommates was a chess instructor and the other two knew how to play the game, but I was only familiar with checkers. Nevertheless, they suggested playing a game of chess. The instructor showed me the basics and though I quickly caught on, I seldom won. I developed a taste for the game, and later purchased a miniature chess set and taught Lue how to play. When the boys were old enough, I taught them and they joined the chess club at school.

All in all, the voyage to England was relaxing and I especially enjoyed the meals. Dinners were an elaborate 'soup to nuts' affair, nothing like we were used to on the base.

After getting settled at Lambourn Downs in Berkshire County, all the pilots were allowed passes to go off base, and London was the first place on our list to see the sights. I particularly enjoyed Madame Trousseau's Wax Museum. Some of the cities were almost demolished. Worst was the inner city of Coventry, which was completely leveled and the walls of a once magnificent church were all that was left standing. I took a taxi tour of the surrounding area to see mile after mile of destroyed homes. Thousands of small incendiary bombs blitzed the cities, their only purpose...burn everything upon contact.

JOHN BRAUCHT

It saddened me to witness the absolute destruction wrought by the Germans. During this time there were no hotels, and the English people would take us into their homes. But since food was strictly rationed, reservations had to be made in advance. The British, who had little to give, shared what they did have with our troops. At this time, the United States had not shipped their planes to England, which meant that the British RAF had to lend us their aircraft. Initially the only planes available for us to train in were called 'Moths'. These small World War I By-Planes, had neither brakes nor tailwheel. The air speed gauge was a flap fastened to the struts between the upper and lower wing. The gas gauge, a stick that protruded from the lower wing worked as a float. The trick, we were told, was to taxi and park the Moth by using blasts of the propeller against the rudder. Then, with the right amount of speed, we could swing the plane into a parking position. Actually the training turned out valuable. Soon the British loaned us Mark IV *Spitfires* with brakes that overheated and could not be used when maneuvering on the ground. We revved up the engine so that the propeller forced enough air against the rudder to steer the plane, the same technique that we learned when training in the Moth. Using this technique, we could maneuver the plane with the rudder instead of brakes.

Our Squadron flew the A-20, a twin engine light bomber that was made in the United States. The A-20, that the British called a DB-7, was the same make of the plane I flew at Key Field. Unfortunately, the runways at Lambourn

A LIFETIME WORTH REMEMBERING

were nothing more than sod fields which made smooth landings almost impossible to make.

We were shown movies and photographs to learn to identify both enemy and ally aircraft. I found a deck of playing cards with silhouettes of most of the aircraft that was used in the war zone. Being able to recognize a plane by silhouette alone was of utmost importance. At great speeds and distances, we could not always determine whether it was our plane or the enemies.

To make matters worse, some of the enemy planes had the same silhouette as ours. If you couldn't tell the difference, you took the chance of downing one of your own planes. I studied the cards and looked for every subtlety.

In addition to being taught survival tactics, we were given a book to study titled *Escape*. Written by a pilot who had been shot down and escaped in enemy territory, it was considered first-hand information.

We were instructed to carry civilian clothing and currency of the area we were to fly over. If we were shot down in the country, our best chance of survival was to find a farm and hide out in the barn or the woods. Then, we were to look for an older person, and attempt to communicate with him that we needed help. The younger generation was not friendly, but older people usually tried to assist the allied teams.

It wasn't much of a choice if we were faced with this situation. Considering the alternatives of being caught, or killed this was overall the wisest thing to do.

A story was passed around about two downed pilots. The first plane was shot down over France. The French

Underground escorted the pilot to safety over the Pyrenees Mountains into Spain. The second pilot went through the same experience a few days later. As fate would have it, the two pilots met in a café in Madrid.

"How come you're still here?" the second pilot asked.

"Because I'm having such a good time, I don't want to leave," the first pilot responded.

One day, while I was flying the Spitfire to familiarize myself with the terrain, I received a call from British control. This came as a complete surprise because it was well known they kept radio silence.

"Flight 624, this is British Air Control."

I picked up my mike. "This is Flight 624 responding. I read you."

"Do you need directions to get to your base?"

"Negative. How do you know my location?"

"We've been tracking your aircraft. You are hereby notified that your unit requests you return to base immediately."

"Is there a problem?" I asked, curious as to why British Air Control would be tracking me.

"Because your Squadron wants you back in time for Christmas dinner."

I laughed. "Thanks. They probably need me to carve the turkey."

I heard the controller laugh. "Well, have a jolly Christmas, Yank."

It was during this period that I met Gene Driscal, an American pilot who became one of my best friends. Our paths would cross many years later.

After the holidays, our unit spent time with an English tank outfit in the event we would later work with them.
 The English tank outfit learned our operation, and we learned their operation. Driving their tanks was an experience. There was no steering wheel. Pulling on the right brake lever turned the tank right and pulling the left lever turned the tank left.

My flight commander sent me on an assignment to the Cambridge Newmarket Airport. I was to learn the RAF's tactics that our squadron was to be involved in. The RAF's mission was to fly low over the English Channel in planes known as Typhoons to any occupied country in West Europe.
 I flew the *Typhoon*, along with a British pilot in another Typhoon, over West Germany. Our mission was to continue until we spotted train tracks, and follow them until we found a freight train. It didn't take long before we saw one. We pulled in broadside and fired at the double boiler engine. Usually the engineer stopped the train, which gave us the advantage of shooting at a still target. Their weapons were different than the Spitfire, which had thirty-caliber weapons with a tracer to zero in on and a twenty-millimeter that blasted massive holes in the 'double boilers'.
 The enemy soon discovered a method to prevent our stratagem and strung cables low across the tracks. After some casualties on our side, orders were changed to correct the situation by flying off to the side.

JOHN BRAUCHT

On our next mission, we managed to disable a second engine by flying to one side. The enemy counteracted this maneuver by building high towers alongside the tracks. This placed us at a disadvantage but we still continued to fly as low as possible. It took the Nazi's considerable time to repair the engines, and thus delayed the movement of war materials.

On my last mission over the Channel, I was flying back to base when I caught sight of three German ME 109's coming up fast behind me. There was no way I could out-fly them. My only recourse was to fly a zigzag maneuver, climb fast and steep and at the same time, make sure I didn't stall. When the plane was high enough, I hit the throttle hard, cut the engine and the plane abruptly slowed down. The 109's on my tail were going too fast to stop, and just as I anticipated, they had no alternative but to whiz right past me.

They swung around and came up again from the rear. By the time the lead plane was ahead of me, I took aim, and my machine gun opened fire. Bulls eye! A barrage of ammo ripped through his left wing. The plane burst into fire, and plunged into the Channel.

"Number one down!" I yelled. "Two to go!"

The second 109 closed in fast on my left. This time, I cut the throttle, and took a nose dive directly for the Channel, skimmed the water and pulled up at the last moment. The 109 was breathing on me. It didn't have a chance to pull out and crashed into the Channel.

"Number two down! One to go!"

Before I had a chance to climb back up, the last 109 caught me on the way up. Bullets tore through the tail, and

A LIFETIME WORTH REMEMBERING

I immediately lost altitude. Smoke was filling the cockpit. I couldn't see and could hardly breathe. I had to bail out. I reached for the canopy lever, gave it one yank, and the canopy flew open.

I bailed out fast and plummeted through the air. I fumbled for the ripcord and gave it a tug. The parachute opened with a jolt then billowed above me. The plane soared through the air for a few moments before it exploded in the distance.

I was a couple of hundred feet from the water when I inflated my 'Mae West' lifejacket and then I ripped off my chute and released the rubber raft that was attached to the seat of my harness and braced myself. I held my breath and sliced through the water feet first. The shock of hitting the icy water almost knocked me out as I went under, but the life jacket's buoyancy brought me up fast.

I broke through the water's surface, gasping for air. By the time I caught my breath, I spotted my raft bobbing up and down just a few yards away. I swam over and climbed inside, exhausted. I fell back in the raft and searched the sky; grateful the third plane wasn't in sight.

The Channel waters were choppy and I was freezing. I felt like a sitting duck in case the 109 decided to take another look. But I considered myself fortunate that I wasn't hurt and counted my blessings. I wasn't in the water long, when I saw the most welcomed sight of a British rescue boat racing toward me. In minutes, I was pulled out of the water.

British radar had picked up my distress and immediately zeroed in on my location.

Since I was flying a British plane, I was awarded a

JOHN BRAUCHT

British medal for bravery in action.

While I was being treated for exposure in the hospital, I heard a story about a not-so-fortunate pilot who tried a victory roll on his return over the squadron area. His engine cut out, his plane went down and he did not survive.

He forgot that the Mark Spitfire had a gravity-feed carburetor, and if he wasn't flying fast enough, or stayed upside down too long, the plane would stall out and crash.

The British DB 7's were similar to the American A 20's. These light twin bombers were used to a lesser degree to slow traffic on overpasses, and to bomb submarine pens at La Harve. Later, *Mustang* P-51's were used by the squadron for escort duty.

One evening I was walking in the mess hall with the flight surgeon, when he turned to me and said, "How long has your voice sounded like that?"

"What do you mean?" I asked.

"I mean that it sounds raspy. Doesn't sound right," he responded. "So how long has it been?"

"Not too long," I replied. My voice has been more hoarse in the last few weeks but I didn't think anything unusual about it.

"Well Braucht, I think you ought to have it looked at. I'd like to admit you to the hospital."

"But, Sir," I said, "It's not that sore and really isn't giving me any trouble."

"It doesn't sound right to me. So I don't think you have a choice, Braucht. You're grounded."

A LIFETIME WORTH REMEMBERING

I was admitted at once to the Oxford General Hospital for a series of tests. The doctors examined me thoroughly but could not diagnose what caused my voice to change. After a series of treatments, they were still unable to bring my speech back to normal. My condition remained the same, and I was not to return to combat duty until they diagnosed the cause of my problem.

While awaiting further orders, I was able to spend time at the college in Oxford. The faculty was extremely kind and loaned me some very old and valuable books. One particular and informative book that I learned much from, was a dictionary that dated back to the translation of the King James Bible. I was also invited to the faculty's homes for dinner on many occasions.

My new orders transferred me to a staging area at High Wycombe where I met the movie star, Gene Raymond. We spent many hours getting to know each other while playing chess. He was an admirable opponent, but I managed to beat him a few times.

My stay at High Wycombe was a short one. I shipped out to Halifax on a Canadian hospital ship carrying hundreds of wounded soldiers. I especially remember one young Canadian soldier who lost his foot in combat.

"How did it happen?" I asked, sensing he wanted to talk about his experience.

"I was in Italy, driving a tank and it seemed like all hell was breaking loose around me when I see this monstrous cannon sticking out of a Nazi tank staring me in the face.

One of those big 90 millimeter babies." He paused to light a cigarette.

"So, what happened then?" I asked.

"Before I could do anything, we got hit. My tank stopped dead and the cab was filling up with smoke. We knew it was going to explode any second, so the only thing we could do was get out fast and head for cover."

"Did they go after you?"

"No. They were too busy chasing our tanks."

I looked down at his bandaged stump. "How did that happen?"

"Well, when I jumped off the tank, I knew I hurt my ankle, but I was so scared, I just kept running until I collapsed in the woods."

He took a deep breath and looked at his leg. "When I woke up I was in an ambulance. They said I must have been in shock when I jumped out of the tank, because my foot was just about completely severed."

"Wow, that must have painful," I said sympathetically.

"No, not then," he added. "I thought maybe I just sprained my ankle when I jumped, but my foot was just hanging on by the tendons."

"So, how do you feel about it now, I mean, losing your foot?"

The Canadian thought for a moment, then shrugged. "It was better than losing my life."

I had no choice but to agree with him. When we embarked at Halifax, I had the opportunity to shake his hand. "I'd like to tell you I think you're a very courageous young man."

A LIFETIME WORTH REMEMBERING

He looked at me with tears in his eyes and said, "Thanks for caring, Yank."

The trip from England to Halifax took about a week. After docking, I took a train to Longview, Texas. I was glad to be back in the good old U.S.A.

I was immediately admitted to the Harman General Hospital, where a specialist ran additional tests on me.

"What we have to do is perform a *Caldwell Lux* on your right antrum," he said.

"What does that mean?" I asked, not liking the sound of what he said.

"In plain English, all it means is, we have to go in and clean out the cavity in your sinus," he explained. "Or to be more exact, to clean out the cavity in your right cheek. It's a relatively simple operation."

"I'm not sure that I want that," I said. "I mean, I'm not hoarse all the time."

"That's not a good enough excuse," he argued.

"What I mean, Sir, is that I'm certain my sinuses acted up because of the cold, damp climate in England. Now that I'm back in the States, especially Texas, I don't have a problem."

The specialist reviewed my chart, then took off his glasses and looked at me. "As far as the Air Force is concerned, young man, you have a problem. And if you don't have the operation, I'm afraid you're going to be grounded permanently. So you don't have much of a choice and neither does the Air Force."

Not wanting to lose my career as a pilot, I consented.

It was only after the operation that I discovered that the doctor did not have the authority to ground me. But by then it was too late.

After a short recuperation in the hospital, I was sent home to Shreveport to wait for a new assignment. I was now attached to Barksdale Field, which was being used as a training base for the B-26. The twin engine *Martin*, which the air force had removed from service and the North American A-26 were designated as the B-26. While I was waiting for my orders, I spent time at the field flying various types of small aircraft to get my flying time requirements.

During that period, we were allowed to take our wives with us when we flew to get in our required hours. One sunny day, I asked Lou, "How would you like to take a ride with me?"

"You mean in the car?" she said.

I laughed. "No, sweetheart, I mean a plane. I need to get my hours in, and I want to get them with the sweetest girl in the world."

She jumped up and gave me a kiss on the cheek. "I'd love to honey!"

That afternoon, we arrived at the base and the only plane available to me was a *Piper Cub*.

Lue pulled back. "It doesn't have any doors, John."

I laughed. "That's because it's a Piper and they don't have them. But it's perfectly safe," I said convincingly.

She looked at me for a long moment. "If you say so."

I helped Lue into the plane and secured her safety belt, then climbed in beside her. With a reassuring smile, I revved the motor. In minutes we were off and in the air.

It was a beautiful day, and Lue indicated that she was enjoying the flight, which up until that time was routine and uneventful. When it was time to return to the base, I veered the plane to the right and Lue was facing the ground.

"I'm afraid, John!" she screamed, shifting her weight in my direction. "I'm going to fall out!"

"No, you won't. It's okay," I assured her. "You're strapped in. You can't fall out."

I leveled the plane and Lue didn't say another word until we landed. In seconds, the safety belt was off and she was out of the plane.

"Don't ever take me in this plane again!" she said, the color slowly coming back to her face.

It took a lot of convincing, but she finally agreed to fly with me again, this time in a twin engine *Cessna* which she felt completely safe in.

Lue and I were now living in a rental apartment and attending the Highland Church. My mother-in-law, Kay, was taking a bible class that was taught by a Jewish teacher of the Levite tribe. He had converted from Judaism to Christianity and subsequently became a Baptist preacher.

"John," Kay said to me one day, "Would you be kind enough to go to class with me tonight?"

"Sure," I said. "Any particular reason?"

"Well, the preacher is teaching us from the Greek manuscript and that's not the way we were taught before. I think that's rather unusual, don't you?"

I was curious as to why he was teaching that method. "Maybe it is," I said. "I'd like to check it out myself."

I attended the next service and was surprised and impressed to discover that the reproduction of the *Codex Sinaiticus*, the preacher was using, was the oldest, most complete and perfect Greek text in use to date. I also learned that the text was not discovered until 1844 and not available until 1868.

I was prepared to find fault with his teachings and checked his text against the words found in the dictionaries I had been given in England. It proved he was using the correct manuscript.

The distribution of the oldest Greek manuscripts to date, was the beginning of furnishing Bible materials to people around the world. This venture turned out to be a labor of love that Lue and I would pursue for the rest of our lives.

I was beginning to feel restless and was constantly hounding Jordan, the Adjutant about my new orders. "When am I going out again," I persisted.

"Don't pester me anymore, John. I'll be the first one to let you know when your orders come in," he said jokingly.

A few weeks later, I was wakened in the middle of the night by a phone call. I jumped up and grabbed the phone. It was my friend Jordan.

"I told you John, that I'd be the first to let you know when your orders came in." He laughed. "So you can come in now and get them."

I looked at the clock. "But Jordan it's two o'clock in the morning."

"Then that'll teach you not to pester me anymore," he said and hung up the phone.

A LIFETIME WORTH REMEMBERING

The next morning, I picked up my assignment from Jordan. In a few days I was in Nashville, training for the Ferry Command. Its function was to deliver aircraft anywhere in the world. I was only there a short time, when I was sent to the 6th Ferry Group in Long Beach. The Pilot Controller asked me if I would make a delivery of an A-35 to Pensacola, Florida on my way to California.

The A-35 was a light single engine bomber with an inverted gull wing. In those days, you were given no prior instructions or training on any particular plane. You just got in, started the engine and took off.

On the way to Pensacola, I thought I would stop off at Barksdale Air Force Base to see my family. I was preparing to land when I noticed a crack directly under my feet. The hair stiffened on my neck. Fire was blowing out of the bomb bay compartment.

I quickly notified the tower of my predicament. By the time they cleared the runway for an emergency landing, I was cutting into the final approach. I hit the runway, and came to a stop as quickly as possible. Flames were starting to shoot up from the floorboard. I was halfway out of the cockpit, when I remembered to switch off the ignition. I got back in and switched it off. If I hadn't, the plane would have exploded.

By the time I made it out on the wing, the firemen were removing the cowling to get at the engine. I jumped to the ground and watched until they had the fire under control.

"You had a gas leak in the engine," the mechanic told me later. "You sure were fortunate you saw the flames when you did, or you would have been one fried flyboy."

When I returned to the base, I was told a P-39, a *Bellaire* single engine pursuit plane had to be delivered to the Russians in Siberia. I accepted the assignment. Early the next morning, I was in the plane and taxiing toward the runway.

"You have permission to take off," the tower reported.

I moved onto the runway, pushed the throttle full force, and started lift off. I was no sooner airborne, than I saw that the nose was too high, which made it impossible to level the plane.

"You have problems 5612," the tower instructed sharply. "Re-enter the pattern."

"Roger," I responded.

"5612, we are clearing the pattern and runway."

At this point there was no alternative but to turn the plane around. I came down tail first.

After the mechanics identified the plane's problem, they said that its cannon was removed and had not been replaced with ballast.

"You can take off as soon as we rectify the problem," the mechanic said.

"Thanks, but no thanks," I said, the memory of the experience still fresh in my mind. "I just got a better offer that I can't resist. I'm going to take a B-24 to Van Ives, California. It's a lot warmer there than Siberia."

After delivering the B-24, I proceeded to Long Beach and reported for duty.

"OSWALD AVERY, COLIN MacLEOD AND MACLYN McCARTHY ISOLATE DNA AS THE HEREDITARY MATERIAL FOR NEARLY ALL LIVING THINGS"

Chapter Twenty-Two
1944

After five years of marriage, Lue and I were expecting our first child. It was difficult during this time for me to get leave but my wife never complained. I wanted to be with her when she went to the hospital, but I wasn't able to make it home until just after our little blue-eyed son was born on April 30th.

We named him Eugene for Eugene Driscal, my best friend in England whom I had flown many missions over enemy territory with, and gave him the middle name Raymond after the movie star Gene Raymond, who I had the pleasure of knowing at High Wycombe.

I bumped into Eugene Driscal a few years later at Patterson Air Force Base in Dayton.

"I want you to know that I named my son John after you," he told me.

I was surprised and said, "Well I'm honored. Thank you very much."

"Your friendship meant a lot to me," he said. "I always knew I could count on you when we were flying."

Although Gene was a wonderful baby, beautiful and seemingly healthy in every respect, it didn't take us long to realize that something was wrong.

"I don't know what to do, John," Lue said, as she put the baby back in the crib. "He won't take more than an ounce of formula at a time and it takes almost an hour to get that into him."

"Maybe that's all he's supposed to," I said, trying to ease her worry, although I was beginning to worry myself.

"No, according to the doctor, he should be drinking at least two ounces by now."

I looked at the clock. It was after three in the morning. We were both pretty worn out, especially Lue. The baby had us up most of the night. "Come on honey, let's go back to bed. You look exhausted. We'll go see the doctor in the morning."

"At first we thought it was colic, or just that he was a fussy baby," Lue said to the doctor, while he was examining Gene.

"And he cries a lot, especially during the night," I added.

"I can hardly get an ounce into him at a time," Lue said.

"Well, first of all," the doctor said, after completing his examination. "Your little Gene is a very healthy young man."

Lue let out a sigh of relief, picked up the baby and cradled him protectively in her arms.

The doctor sat down at his desk. "It's nothing to worry

A LIFETIME WORTH REMEMBERING

about, but your baby is what we call tongue-tied."

Lue gasped. "What does that mean?"

"Relax Mrs. Braucht. All that means is the child can't swallow because there's a shortening of the frenuum below his tongue, which puts a terrible amount of effort on its ability to swallow. Usually they are exhausted before they drink enough to be satisfied. That's why he cries a lot." He looked at little Gene in Lue's arms. "Poor little tyke. He's always hungry and can't get full."

"What can you do about it?" I asked.

"We'll just clip the little membrane under the tongue and that should do the trick."

Lue held the baby closer. "Is it a dangerous operation, Doctor?"

He smiled. "Well no operation is without its risks, but I can assure you, this is a very safe and simple procedure."

The doctor did the operation in his office and within a few days, Gene was able to swallow with less difficulty. He grew strong and healthy in spite of the fact that he was never able to drink much more than two ounces of formula at one time.

By the time Gene outgrew his bottle, he was eating and drinking without a problem.

It was during the hottest days of summer when we left Shreveport to move to California. Our car didn't have an air conditioner and by the time we pulled in to Albuquerque, the temperature was over a hundred degrees in the shade. The baby was sweaty and crying, and Lue was almost overcome with the heat.

JOHN BRAUCHT

We thought it best to stay at a motel until nighttime and drive when it was cooler.

Lue and I arrived in Long Beach, and stayed with my Aunt Nell and her family for about a month until we were able to find an apartment near the base.

Although we saw the Los Angeles Rose Parade many times we never tired of seeing the magnificent floats that were covered with millions of roses.

We even visited Forest Lawn Cemetery, which most people think of as a tourist sight. It was especially appealing to me because my early childhood was spent in the stone and marble industry. At first glance, we were impressed with the beautifully manicured grounds, but found the workmanship of the marble and granite statues and crypts in the magnificent mausoleums unparalleled. Lue was more impressed with the stained glass windows of the chapel, and the depiction of the Last Supper. Many of the mausoleums held the final remains of movie stars and famous people.

We also visited a building in Los Angeles, where Mr. Knoch the great Greek scholar and translator of the Bible held his classes, using the printing of the oldest available Greek text discovered in 1844.

When I was flying around the states, I took the Greek text with me to many universities. I discussed this text with the professors at the universities and presented them with a copy.

The response from the majority of the professors was that the Greek text was void of contradiction and the workmanship excellent.

A LIFETIME WORTH REMEMBERING

I reported back to duty and my assignment was to deliver a B-17G to Tulsa, Oklahoma, followed by another assignment to Rapid City, Iowa and still another to Denver, Colorado. During my station at Long Beach, I ferried just about every combat and transport aircraft there was.

Initially, we were told, "There it is, deliver it". but later they made us read all the Tech Orders, with final requirement to co-pilot the aircraft with a qualified pilot.

All types of aircraft had to be delivered to all parts of the world. Most deliveries were safe and routine, but flying the P-38's, with the quiet in-line engines, sometimes proved to be dangerous. If one engine failed on take off and you didn't cut the other back quickly and adjust the trim, the plane would flip over. We lost several planes because the pilots didn't cut back and adjust the trim fast enough.

The first delivery I made in the P38 was from Long Beach to Newark, with two stops at Albuquerque and Belleville, Illinois. After being stationed in England, I knew first hand how badly oversea pilots needed the P38s, so whenever the opportunity presented itself, I was eager and ready to deliver them. At one time I delivered one P38 every day for three consecutive days. I was able to accomplish this by taking a commercial flight back to base at night. This way I could get caught up on my sleep.

I was flying a P-38 out of Albuquerque when I made a decision to climb to twenty thousand feet rather than the usual low-level flight. This way I would move into the jet stream and get more miles to the gallon. After I reached the required altitude, I looked around for an oxygen mask, which I was required to use. Unfortunately, the plane was not equipped with one. Usually there was no oxygen in the new P-38's. This time, there was oxygen but no mask. I made do by taking the tube that should have been attached to the mask, and put it directly into my mouth. It worked fine.

Air and Airway Communication Service (AACS) must have passed my flight plan to Air Traffic Control (ATC).

"You cannot fly from Albuquerque to New Jersey without refueling," Air Traffic Control advised me.

"I've got a high tail wind and I'm making good ground speed. I think everything is A OK. Thanks anyway."

When I arrived at New Jersey I had plenty of fuel to spare.My calculations were correct.

It was during a subsequent flight to New Jersey, that the most frightening experience in my life occurred. I took off without a hitch and climbed to twenty thousand feet.

The P-38 was equipped with a new type of booster control to make the plane easier to handle with a warning, "turn off the booster control if rough air is anticipated".

I decided to test the booster control and turned it on. They were right. The plane flew like a dream. I could handle it with my little finger.

For a while everything went fine, but suddenly it started to get rough. I was caught in a down draft and the plane flipped upside down. Before I had the chance to right it, the plane went into a flat downward spin.

I shut off the booster control and looked at the altimeter. My heart almost stopped beating. I had fallen almost 5000 feet, and the ground was coming up fast. By now, I

A LIFETIME WORTH REMEMBERING

was perspiring and my heart was about to come through my chest.

I knew the odds of pulling out of a spin were poor and glanced at the altimeter again. By now I was down almost 7000 feet. I played with the rudder pedals and the ailerons at the same time, until the plane turned right side up and came out of the spin.

I breathed a sigh of relief, thankful that God was with me and completed my mission without further incident.

My next job was to ferry a P-38 from Long Beach to El Paso, Texas. I was on my way to Coolidge, Arizona under Visual Flight Rules (VFR) to refuel, when I realized that I had left my briefcase with all my charts and manuals behind. After I left for El Paso, I was now under Instrument Flight Rules (IFR) only until I was within a few miles to the airport. Then my only choice was to continue the flight by relying on experience and instinct. As I approached the airport, I was instructed to descend under Visual Flight Rules.

It was on the fourth of July when the time came for me to be checked out in the A-26, a twin engine light bomber, which was equipped with just one set of controls. I sat next to the pilot in a jump seat, and observed his every move. After a routine flight, he landed the plane and turned off the ignition.

"Now you fly it," he said, climbing out of the cockpit.

"Aren't you going to fly with me?" I asked.

He grinned, and gave me a high sign. "Nope. You're on your own, Braucht."

I slid over to the pilot's seat, turned on the engine, hit the throttle and prepared for take off. Everything went off without a hitch and I was now underway, heading for Savanna, Georgia.

I had to fly high above the clouds because I was under Visual Flight Rules (VFR) which in plain English meant, 'stay where you can see and be seen'. This B-26B was not equipped with a radio compass and since I was above the clouds with no means of navigating, I was flying by experience and gut instinct.

By the time I arrived over the eastern coastline, it was dark and I could make out the lights of a city below. I dropped to a lower altitude and was relieved to see I was flying over a large airport.

"Are you lost?" the airport tower queried.

"No, but what airport is this?"

"Charleston," they replied. "You are over Charleston Airport. You better land if you're lost."

"I'm not lost now," I said. "My destination is Savanna."

I was very relieved when I reached Savanna, which was only a short distance along the coast. That flight was the furthest destination I ever missed while I was navigating. Either I was extremely fortunate or I had the navigation instincts of a bird.

While we were learning to fly the A-26 twin-engine light bomber, the Checkout Instructor's last words were, "Make sure you latch both sides of the canopy before you take off. A lot of guys forgot to do this, and lost the canopies." He shook his head. "And let me tell you, the Air Force isn't

A LIFETIME WORTH REMEMBERING

very happy when that happens."

I completed training a few days later and was preparing for take off. I climbed into the sleek twin engine, and turned on the engine. Everything sounded great and I had no sooner left the ground, than a gush of air hit me in the face.

Then I heard the dreaded sound of flapping. It was the canopy. To my horror, I realized that I had only latched the left side.

I reached outside and grabbed the rim of the canopy with one hand, grabbed the mike with the other and contacted the tower.

"Requesting an immediate landing!" I yelled. Perspiration dripped down my face and I was fighting to keep the canopy down. My arm felt like it was being torn off.

"What's the problem?" the tower responded.

"I'm losing my canopy!" I yelled back.

"We're clearing the pattern and runway for an emergency landing."

I dropped the mike on my lap, pushed the throttle full speed, and grabbed the stick, all the time struggling to hang on to the canopy.

I made a smooth landing, grateful that the plane and I were still intact. I moved off the runway, and with my hand still glued to the canopy, came to a complete stop. I slowly let go of the canopy, and slumped in the seat. My legs and arms were shaking beyond control.

"Are you okay?" the tower inquired.

"Yes," I managed to mumble.

"Do you need any assistance?"

"No, I just need to get my heart out of my feet."

I sat there and considered myself very fortunate that I hadn't wrecked the plane, as it would have been a costly error on my part.

After a few minutes, I made sure that both sides of the canopy were securely latched, then called the tower.

"Request taxi instruction for take off again," I said.

"Make sure you're latched in this time."

Not only did I make sure that I was bolted in, but from that day on, I double-checked the flight instructions before I took off.

My next ferry was to deliver an A-26 to Valley Wales in the United Kingdom. The plane's tank didn't hold enough fuel to make a direct flight, so I refueled at Texas, Georgia, Maine, then Goose Bay, Labrador in North East Canada, then Greenland, Iceland and finally on to Valley Wales. This route was used in the summer months and the south Atlantic route was used in the winter because of inclement weather.

The only time I ever flew in a group of A-26's was from Goose Bay. All the planes were lined up; ready for take off, when we received orders from air control to stop the engines.

I looked up and spotted a wing spiraling through the sky, followed by a British *Mosquito* plummeting earthward in a flat spin. In seconds, the plywood plane crashed into a nearby field and exploded.

The pilot was swaying from side to side as he parachuted down in the direction of the runway. Two pilots raced toward him, holding a jacket between them, to help break his fall. Fortunately, before they could reach him, he landed

A LIFETIME WORTH REMEMBERING

safely on the soft side of the runway.

We later heard that the pilot wasn't wearing his chute in the plane. Just before he bailed out, he grabbed it and held it against his chest. When he pulled the ripcord, the nylon shrouds ripped his face to shreds. He had to have extensive plastic surgery to reconstruct his face.

"At least I'm alive," he told the surgeon. "My engineer wasn't so fortunate. He froze at the last minute and went down with the plane."

Our next stop was B W Air Base One in Greenland. I knew it was going to be a difficult flight because the hillsides surrounding the narrow fjords gave the illusion of tunnel vision. We studied films that pointed out the exact route to take to avoid a crash. Once you entered the fjord, there were two routes that formed a "Y". We were instructed to take the left fjord at the junction. I followed the guidelines and made a perfect landing on the steepest runway I ever came across.

Greenland had the biggest mosquitoes I ever saw. They reminded me of a tale I heard about the mosquitoes in the Louisiana bayous. It seems as though a fellow went to sleep, and the next morning when he awoke, the mosquitoes had eaten his mule and were pitching horseshoes to see who would wear the harness.

I decided to spend the rest of the afternoon climbing a glacier.

I was delivering an A-26 to Ascension Island in the South Atlantic and well warned of the landing dangers there.

"You are to come in high and fast, Braucht," the

Operation Officer said. "That runway presents an even bigger problem. "You're going to have to land practically on a dime."

"A dime?" I questioned.

"Well, to be more accurate let me describe it as landing on a ledge. You have a sharp drop at the entry of the runway, another drop at the end, and to make matters worse, one on the left."

"That doesn't sound too difficult," I said.

He grinned at me. "I'm not finished yet, Braucht. Guess what's on your right?"

I shrugged. "I don't have a clue."

"How about a cliff that runs the length of the runway like a wall?"

Before I could comment, he added, "And don't forget about the down drafts. You remember the Mosquito that was caught in one? He crashed into that very cliff."

Armed with all the information and the dangers ahead of me, I was preparing for take off, when I learned that another pilot was heading for Ascension Island at the same time.

"How about you flying high altitude?" he suggested, as we went over our flight plans.

"Sure," I said, "Either way's okay with me but how come you want to fly low? They say it's more dangerous."

He grinned. "You got that right. And I intend to fly this baby right through with no problems and break a new speed record."

"So, I guess you're planning to get there before me."

He laughed. "You'll be eating my dust."

I was well aware that he had a reputation for being a

hotshot pilot, and I wasn't looking to win any race but I had already checked out the wind and speed, and knew that a higher altitude and descent would give me the advantage of increased speed.

And I was right. By the time he arrived at the Island, I was already in the mess hall, half way through dinner.

"Get caught in a dust storm?" I asked, trying not to rub it in.

"I had some engine problems," he growled.

My next stop was Roberts Air Base at Monrovia in Liberia, Africa. While there, I visited the rubber plantations. Many of the slaves returned to Monrovia after Lincoln abolished slavery. Some of these slaves were educated while held captive in the states and they used that education to become successful in government and business.

From Monrovia, I went to Dakar, Senegal, then on to Marrakech, Morocco where my crew and I went sightseeing. We stumbled across a museum, which was once a notorious *seraglio* owned by a sultan.

When in use, each concubine was given her own room that wasn't much bigger than a walk-in closet. The toilets were nothing more than a hole in the floor. A large stone wall embedded with jagged glass shards surrounded the harem to discourage intruders.

On my second trip to Marrakech, I was surprised to find Harry, one of my pilots, in the Base Operations hanger. My schedule was hectic and it didn't give me time to check out where my pilots were at all times, and I was not notified by On-Duty personnel that Harry had not returned to base in the allotted time. In fact, he had been there for a week.

"Why are you still here?" I inquired.

"I had a lot of engine trouble," he responded.

I suspected he wasn't being truthful and was having himself a vacation. "Well," I said, "you get that engine fixed and get yourself back to base pronto."

This excuse was used by a lot of guys when they wanted to get a little extra 'R & R'. It was somewhat overlooked, as their excuses couldn't be proven and no real harm was done.

After Morocco, we delivered the A-26's to Valley Wales in Britain, then flew military transport back to Long Beach.

I couldn't wait to see my wife and child. Gene was almost a year old and would have been the envy of any girl with his natural curly flaxen hair, fair complexion and big blue eyes. Even though he was mistaken for a girl several times, Lue was reluctant to cut his long curls.

I was pushing Gene in his carriage through the neighborhood one morning, when two ladies stopped to admire him.

"What a beautiful little girl," the taller one said.

"She certainly is," the other agreed. "Just look at those blonde ringlets and blue eyes. She's a real little beauty."

"I hate to disagree with you ladies," I said, "but this beautiful little girl is my handsome little son."

"I don't believe it," they both said, bending over to take a closer look at Gene.

I laughed. "I think my wife and I are quite capable of telling the difference between a boy and a girl."

"Well, he should be a girl. He's too pretty to be a boy," the taller one insisted.

When I got home, I told Lue what the women had said, and we both agreed that the time had come for Gene to get his first haircut. After that, no one mistook him for a girl again.

I was pretty fortunate that I was never away any longer than twenty-seven days at a time so I was able to see my family often.

I was home about two weeks, when I was on my way again with another A-26 heading for Roberts AFB.

I was given a copy of the AAF Air Transport Command Sixth Ferrying Division book by the Commanding Officer. It contained photographs of personnel and airplanes from the early days of the Wright Brothers to present day, job classifications by rank, the history of aviation and photographs and articles about Barbara Jane Erickson Squadron Leader of the WASP Operations. I've had many occasions to refer to the book, which proved to be beneficial in my career.

I assumed my next position with the Fifty Second Ferrying Squadron shortly after arriving at Long Beach. I was transferred to Pilot Control with Major Ben M. Adams in Unit Command. This section was part of a base operation that assigned pilots to make deliveries around the world. This would prove to be a choice position. I was allowed to choose any destination and fly any aircraft that I chose.

Colonel Bradley became our new Commanding Officer.

He rarely kept an eye on us and there was no one else in charge.

Some of the officers complained to Colonel Bradley that they were unhappy about the hours in our schedule.

"You men can work out your own problems," the Colonel said.

Later in the afternoon, we got together and held a meeting. Everyone made suggestions that no one agreed. I waited until they ran out of suggestions, and said, "I have an idea."

"You have the floor," one of the complaining officers said. "Anything's got to be better than the schedule we have now."

"Okay then," I said, "How about it gentlemen, if each one of us draft up a schedule, then we'll all look them over and take a vote."

The men thought that it was a good idea, and before the day was over, we worked out a scheduled agreeable to everyone.

When the Colonel heard how we handled the problem, I was put in charge.

The only hitch was that I was a First Lieutenant and there was one Captain who resented taking orders from anyone below his rank. He informed the Colonel that he refused to work for me. The Colonel then resolved the matter. "I'm promoting you to captain, Braucht."

From then on, I had no problems with the men.

I received a call from a police sergeant in Savanna, Georgia, regarding a problem with a Flight Officer.

"We're holding one of your men here," the Sergeant said.

"What did he do?" I asked.

"He's charged with drunk and disorderly conduct."

"May I speak with him?"

The Sergeant put the Flight Officer on the phone. "Look," I said, "I don't want to get into any details now, but if they let you go, you get yourself back to Long Beach immediately."

"Yes, sir," he said.

"What do you want us to do with the guy?" the Sergeant said, getting back on the phone.

I thought about it a moment, and said, "I sure would appreciate it Sergeant, if you'd release him on his own recognizance."

To prevent a situation like this from happening again, I decided to implement a new procedure and called a briefing.

"All pilots will be required to send this unit a telegram every day," I said, handing out written instructions. "You will need to give us your location and reason for being there. You will now use the code RON which indicates Remaining Over Night. RON #1 will indicate a Regular Stop. We have approximately eight RON codes, each representing a different problem that might occur, for example engine trouble is RON #2, bad weather RON #3, et cetera."

As a result of this procedure, we had excellent control of each pilot and aircraft's whereabouts and condition in the United States.

At this time, I was ferrying mostly C-46-D's in the United States and all over the world. On one particular flight, I ferried the P-61 known as the *Black Widow*, which was a twin boom aircraft like the P-38. A number of Barbara Jane Erickson's squadron had delivered these slow and clumsy black planes that were difficult to detect at night. These women pilots were members of the Women's Air Force Service Pilots. WASP was disbanded in 1944, but I had the pleasure of meeting Barbara while she was still Squadron Commander.

Chapter Twenty-Three
WINTER 1944

My next assignment turned out to be a most interesting and unforgettable one. I was to escort celebrities around the world where they were to perform for the servicemen.

Bob Hope flew with me several times and I found him to be extremely personable, down to earth and funny. On one occasion when we were heading for a performance, Bob, who I was now on a first name basis with, was getting on the plane sporting a bottle of whiskey. I was surprised to hear him talking loud, and he appeared to have 'tied one on'.

"I'm sorry, Bob," I said politely, "but I'm afraid you can't take that whiskey on board."

He laughed and waved the bottle at me. "I have a cold and the doctor prescribed it for me. How about you soldier, don't you need something for what ails you?"

I refused and figured he must have been pretty scared and needed a drink to give him courage. A lot of guys thought that drinking helped.

Jerry Colonna flew with me a couple of times. He was a quiet kind of guy with his nose stuck in a book most of the flight. He wasn't anything like the loud-mouthed comic he portrayed in the movies.

Vera Vague was very sweet and had the smoothest skin I had ever seen, that is, with the exception of my lovely wife

Dinah Shore Montgomery, who was married to George Montgomery at the time, was a soft spoken and genteel southern lady, and every bit as pleasant as her on-screen personae.

For some reason that I still cannot understand, people thought I resembled William Bendix. I've had many people approach me, but the time that sticks out in my mind the most, was when a woman stopped me while I was walking along the street.

"May I have your autograph, Mr. Bendix?" she said.

"I'm sorry," I responded, "I think you have the wrong person."

"You're not William Bendix the movie star?" she said.

"No ma'am, I'm not."

"Well I say you are," she insisted.

I decided not to argue with her, since her mind apparently was made up.

Unfortunately, I never stayed in any one place long enough to see the entertainers perform on stage.

It was December 24th, 1944 and we were given last minute instructions to fly C-46's to Hawaii. Another Christmas I'd miss spending with my family. Lue was disappointed that I wouldn't be there for Gene's first Christmas but she understood, as usual.

After seven hours en route, we were ordered to return to home base, because the weather was bad in Hawaii and landing there would be dangerous.

JOHN BRAUCHT

"HIROSHIMA IS ATTACKED AUGUST 6TH WITH AN ATOMIC BOMB, AND THE JAPANESE SURRENDER ON SEPTEMBER 2ND."

Chapter Twenty-Four
1945

We took off again for Hawaii on New Year's eve and for the second time in a week had to return to base because of bad weather. We tried for the third time on January 3rd and this time we carried enough tanks of fuel to last the long trip to Hawaii.

But we still had problems. It was cold and the engineer couldn't get the heater to work. He was unfamiliar with the C-46's new heating system. By the time he figured out how to get it working, he had pumped too much gas overboard.

I calculated how much gas was left, and had no choice but to pull the throttle back and slow the plane down to a point where we were barely air-born. This was the only way to conserve our fuel supply.

It took us a record fifteen hours and thirty-five minutes before we arrived at John Rogers Airport in Hawaii. We were put up overnight in a Quonset hut not far from the runway. The only facilities to wash up were outside in back of the building. My co-pilot and I went outside to wash up when we heard a plane flying directly overhead.

At first glance it looked like a transport plane but upon closer inspection, we realized it was a twin rudder B-24 converted to a single rudder.

The plane was coming in fast and low, smoke pouring out of the cockpit. At about twenty-five feet from the ground, a door opened and two men jumped out, bounced off the runway and tumbled almost forty feet. Both of them died upon impact. The pilot and co-pilot were sticking with the plane. Just as it was about to land on the runway, it stalled, smashed into the ground, split in half and killed the pilot and co-pilot. To everyone's amazement, a dog trotted out of the fuselage, none the worse for his experience.

On February 19th, I started out from Oakland, California for Hawaii, Canton, Trawa, Guadal Canal and Biak. From there I hopped a shuttle to Townsville, Australia to take a B-25 back to the states. Heavy cannons were mounted in the front part of the B-25's fuselage. When the cannons were fired, they caused so much damage to the planes, they had to be returned for repairs.

I had just left Townsville when the plane started giving me trouble. The engine kept cutting in and out. I landed in Tontouta and was tempted to abandon the plane. Instead, I stayed an extra day while the mechanics tried to repair the engine.

The next morning I was en route to the Fiji Islands. The right engine still presented a problem, but I managed to land safely in a small beautiful island in the southwest Pacific. The Melanesian natives were friendly, and both men and women wore nothing but sarongs.

I took off for Hamilton Air Force Base in San Francisco by way of Canton, Christmas Island and Hawaii. By the time I reached Canton, every thing was running smooth. Our last hop was to Christmas Island and Hawaii.

When I was coming in on the final approach, the plane ran out of fuel. Fortunately, we were high enough to glide onto the runway without a hitch but the plane had to be towed to the hangar.

Most of the flights I took in the past were for combat and a few transports like the twin engine C-47 and C-46. Now I started to fly larger bombers and transports like the four engine B-29 and the four engine C-54 and C-74.

We usually rode a transport craft back from ferry delivery. When in the United States, we used civilian airlines and had a Number Two priority. The President and his cabinet had Number One.

I was returning to base from Australia, when a Brigadier General climbed on board and took a seat alongside me. After we had exchanged a few pleasantries, I commented, "I'm surprised you're taking one of these transports back to the states."

"I'm not that important," he joked. "Actually, I was bumped off an earlier flight by one of your airmen."

I wasn't home long when I was off again to Biak, a small island on the eastside of West New Guinea. The Japanese had tunneled through a steep embankment from one end to the other. U.S. troops were closing in on a small outfit trapped at the furthest end of the tunnel. The trapped Japanese were resisting, but they were slowly being wiped out by the time I arrived at the scene.

I was given permission to look around the entrance of the tunnel. As I wandered about inside, I saw small openings in the walls.

"The Japs shot at us from those holes," a soldier said.

Inside the tunnel, the area was covered with Japanese mortar shells. I picked up a couple for souvenirs.

I gave one to my uncle that he made into a lamp. When I suggested to Lue that we do the same, she laughed.

"Somehow, John, I don't believe that thing would match our décor."

I was en route to Hawaii in a C-46 when I realized that our compass was off seven degrees. "Check the degrees out," I told the young navigator. "And be sure and make the proper changes."

When it was almost time to arrive at our destination, the navigator reported, "I'm sorry, but I don't know where we are."

"What corrections did you make?" I asked.

"Half of what the compass was off," he said.

"Why didn't you make the full correction?" I demanded to know.

"I didn't think it was that bad," he said.

I calculated the compass. "Don't you realize that we're about 300 miles south of Hawaii and we should be heading north?"

A LIFETIME WORTH REMEMBERING

He shook his head apologetically and went back to his seat, leaving me to rectify his mistake. I banked the plane north, got back on course, and flew by radio beams. It took us two hours longer to reach our destination because of this error.

The Hump, a narrow gap between two Burmese Mountain ranges, made take off and landing in India most dangerous, especially when clouds covered the gap. I was fortunate that it was a clear day when I flew through the ranges.

Our mission was to supply B-29 bombers to troops fighting in the India Burma War. Troops from the United States, Burma and China were fighting the Japanese. We delivered pursuit aircraft to General Claire Chennault, Commander of the Flying Tigers in China, where they were to be used to fight the Japanese Air Force who were stationed both in Japan and in China.

JOHN BRAUCHT

"JOHN MAUCHLY AND JOHN ECKERT FINISH ENIAC, THE FIRST ALL-PURPOSE COMPUTER THAT HAS VACUUM TUBES TO DISPLAY DECIMAL NUMERALS"

Chapter Twenty-Five
1946

The war now over, many of our flights were to deliver aircraft to storage silos located in the southwest. When we approached Bush Field in Augusta, Georgia, my crew started stripping all the instruments.

"What are you doing?" I said. "You don't have any business taking those things."

"If we don't take it, the civilians will as soon as we leave the plane," one of my men said. "And they get to sell it."

"That doesn't give you the right to steal."

"We don't consider it stealing," another crewman popped up. "They're not going to use this stuff anymore."

I shrugged. It really wasn't any of my business, and I wasn't even sure there was a rule to prevent it.

JOHN BRAUCHT

I returned to Long Beach and went to see the Adjutant. When I entered his office, he was glancing through a stack of files.

"Have a seat, John," he said.

I pulled up the chair "You sent for me?"

He put the papers down and stacked them in a neat pile.

"Yes. I've just been given orders to discharge about a thousand pilots."

He must have noticed the surprised expression on my face, and quickly added, "Don't worry, John. You're not one of them. As a matter of fact how would you like to work with Air Force Weather personnel?"

"That would be great," I said, breathing a sigh of relief. "Where do you intend to send me?"

He opened a manila file and scanned through the papers. "What about Headquarters, Air Force Base Weather at Andrews Air Force Base?"

"You mean Gravely Point?"

"That's right, Washington, D.C., the nation's capital."

A LIFETIME WORTH REMEMBERING

"EDWIN LAND INVENTS THE POLAROID LAND CAMERA"

Chapter Twenty-Six
1948

I was extremely pleased with the course of events my life was taking. As Ranking Officer, my new assignment was to set up requirements for weather stations in the early warning areas of northern Canada. My responsibility was to figure out what equipment would be required. This was an area that I was totally unfamiliar with.

I enlisted the help of an experienced officer, and researched the library to give me the information I needed. Within a few weeks, I gathered enough data to initiate the operation. The books mapped out in detail everything required for the weather stations. Fortunately, I didn't have to know if the equipment would work or not...all I had to know were names and numbers.

While Lue and I were living in Washington D.C, our six-year-old had gotten into Grandma Kay's jewelry box. Later, she discovered her earrings were missing.

"Gene," she said, "tell Grandma what you did with her earrings?"

"I hid them," he admitted with a mischievous look on his face.

"Where did you hide them?" Grandma Kay asked

"I don't wanna tell," he said.

"If you don't tell me where they are, I'm afraid I'm going to have to punish you."

"Then I'll run away," he said bravely.

Grandma Kay was pretty smart, and wanted to teach him a lesson and call his bluff. She winked at Lue, who was observing everything from the doorway. "Okay," she said, "I'll even help you pack."

Looking a little bewildered, Gene marched into his room and grabbed his hat and coat.

Grandma Kay took a suitcase out of the closet and tossed it on the bed.

"You're going to need more clothes than that. How are you going to sleep?"

Grandma Kay and Lue opened his drawer and took out underwear, pajamas, a couple of shirts and filled the suitcase. "Now you can leave."

He walked out of the house under the watchful eye of Lue and Grandma Kay. When he reached the corner of the house, he sat on the curb, with his elbows on his knees and his fists under his chin for a few minutes. Then he peeked over his shoulder and seeing that no one was coming after him, he got up and came back in the house.

"Aren't you going to run away?" Lue asked him.

"I changed my mind," he said, looking a little less

A LIFETIME WORTH REMEMBERING

courageous than he did earlier.

"Oh," Grandma Kay said. "And why is that?"

He sighed and lowered his head. "Because I didn't know where to go."

"In that case, Gene, do you remember now where you hid my earrings?"

"Yes, Grandma, they're under the paper over there," he said, pointing to the corner of the room.

"What paper?" Lue said.

"Over in the corner," he said sheepishly.

Grandma Kay held back a giggle. "He means under the wall paper, where he has to stand when he's naughty."

Sure enough, Lue found Grandma Kay's earrings tucked snuggly behind a small strip of loosened wallpaper that Gene had picked at over a period of time.

Later, Grandma Kay painted a picture of Gene sitting on the sidewalk, which she gave to him.

Upon the successful completion of my job at Andrews, I was sent to Air Force Air Weather Headquarters at the Pentagon. Colonel Moreland, who later became General Moreland was in charge of this assignment. My assignment was to build up personnel in weather forecasting. After the war, the military was so busy discharging personnel that they ran short of weathermen.

My first task was to check all personnel files and contact as many men as possible. The intent was to save time and money by getting these well-trained and experienced men back in the service for Air Weather jobs.

The problem was that fine line ink drawings and small

printing on extremely large maps were almost impossible to read, and was causing eye sight strain on the men, so I got a waiver to lower eye vision requirements from 30/30 to 40/40.

Eventually we were successful in getting students to enroll in Weather School, by promising them a four-year college education. That is, if they completed a four-year hitch in the military.

By this time I had moved my family to Easton, Pennsylvania because the cost of living was lower there. Each weekend, I drove my little *Nash Rambler* 600 home. The Rambler was not a fast car, and I was careful not to exceed the speed limit especially when I drove through Maryland. It had a reputation of being a notorious speed trap. Nevertheless, one day I heard a siren coming up fast behind me, and I pulled over. I waited until an officer got out of his car and came over to me.

"What did I do officer?" I asked, fully aware that I had not been speeding.

"You were doing fifty-five miles per hour in a fifty mile per hour zone," he said, pulling out his ticket book.

"But officer," I said. "I'm sure I was doing under fifty."

He gave me a look that said he didn't care. "I clocked you at fifty-five, he said. Now you can either come down to the court house and fight it, or pay the eighteen dollar fine now."

I knew it wouldn't do me any good to go to the courthouse, so I thought it more prudent to pay the fine and leave it at that.

After that episode, I made it a point to pick up college students when I was going north and military hitchhikers when I was heading south. In exchange for the ride, I asked them to watch the speedometer and make sure I didn't go over the speed limit.

The police stopped me almost every time I went through the speed trap, and fortunately I had witnesses in the car who could prove that I was not speeding.

"You stop me in this trap for speeding every time I pass through," I told an officer. "I intentionally pick up hitchhikers so that they can watch my speedometer and tell me if I'm doing over fifty."

He looked in the car at a young soldier I had picked up.

"Yes, sir, officer," the soldier said. "He was only doing forty-five miles."

The officer gave us a dirty look and said, "Hmm...okay, go ahead."

Lue and I decided it was time to buy a house in Washington D.C. area, so we could be near each other. We looked around Virginia and found a two-bedroom modest home for twelve thousand dollars.

The owner wanted cash, so I went to the bank and withdrew the money and paid off the entire mortgage.

For the first month everything was working out fine and I got to see Lue and Gene every day. We were just about settled when my sinuses began acting up.

The condition continued to plague me, worse than it had been in England. The pain finally became unbearable and I requested a transfer to a drier climate. My job at the Pentagon was finished and even though Colonel Moreland wanted me to stay, the cold northern winters were not agreeing with me.

I was on a small military shuttle boat, and had the opportunity to meet and talk with General Lamay, Commander of the Air Force.

Three positions were available to me. I chose Montgomery, Alabama because of the climate.

Lue and I were given quarters on Maxwell Field. The house was in a good location and we were allowed to decorate at will. We became friendly with a Colonel and his wife, who lived next door. They had a little male black Cocker Spaniel, and we had a blonde female Cocker. The two dogs got together and fell in love. Before long we were the proud parents of six black purebred puppies. When they were ten weeks old, all were sold but the runt. Our cleaning man, whose dog had just died, gave us twenty-five silver dollars for the runt.

The apartment now decorated, we were settling into a normal life style when our second son came along on November 27th, 1948. Lue named him Ricky after one of her favorite characters in a novel and Bryan, Dad's middle name who was named after William Jennings Bryan, the great political leader.

Again we were blessed with a beautiful baby. He was perfect in every respect, but immediately after his birth, we learned he had a broken collarbone.

"But how did that happen?" Lue was quick to ask.

A LIFETIME WORTH REMEMBERING

"It happens quite often during the delivery," the doctor informed us. "And I assure you that it is nothing to be concerned about."

"Was it something I did?" Lue asked.

"No, no," the doctor said. "Rest assured you did everything right."

"But how will it heal?" she continued.

"Do you have to set it?" I asked.

"No, nothing that drastic," the doctor answered. "Mother Nature will take care of it."

"So, what are we supposed to do?" I said. "I mean, how do we take care of him so we don't hurt him."

"Be careful when you pick him up. Make sure there's no stress near his collarbone. Carry him around on a pillow and his weight will be evenly distributed."

We were pretty careful when we picked him up, and after carrying him around on the pillow for three months, Ricky's collarbone completely mended, as the doctor said it would.

Gene was very proud of his little brother and liked showing him off.

"Don't get too close," he'd warn his friends. "We don't want to get germs on him."

Lue stayed pretty busy taking care of the boys and the house. Whenever I had a day off, I'd mind them while Lue went shopping. As soon as she left, I'd start thumbing through a collection of favorite recipes, which were made into a cookbook by a group of personnel wives. By the time Lue returned home, I'd have dinner on the table, and the boys bathed and dressed for bed.

Sometimes Lue and the boys went to the lowering of the

flag ceremony at sunset, and listen to the military band at Maxwell Field.

By 1948, the Air Force was monitoring all military aircraft for safety. This was a 24-hour operation and was done in three eight-hour shifts. During the war, the men worked a seven-day week, but now that it was peacetime, the officers at Maxwell Air Force Base had more time off. We took turns working a progressive shift. Fridays were the busiest and Sundays the slowest because traffic was spread out more.

Pilots were required to fly a designated number of hours each month, in order to justify their pay. My job as CheckOut Pilot was to teach the pilots how to fly the specific type of aircraft they needed for qualification.

I was flying an officer to Denver for a special meeting. The A-26 had a glass nose cone, where the bombardier sat when the plane was used during the war. The only other seat was next to the pilot. The officer rode beside me and an enlisted man sat in the nose.

I was flying a little high when the Denver tower gave me a straight-in approach. To compensate, I had to make a very steep descent with the nose pointed almost perpendicular to the ground. The landing was smooth and without incident.

I climbed out and walked toward the front of the plane. "You can open the hatch and come out now," I said to the enlisted man.

He nodded, made an attempt to open the floor hatch, then turned and crawled through the plane and climbed out of the canopy in the pilot's seat. He looked pale and leaned

A LIFETIME WORTH REMEMBERING

against the plane taking deep breaths.

"Check out the nose hatch," I told a mechanic who was approaching the plane.

The mechanic climbed back out and nodded toward the enlisted man. "There's a mess in there. The guy got sick."

"What happened?" I asked the enlisted man, whose color was starting to return to his face.

"I'm sorry sir, he said, his eyes filling with fear. "But I fell asleep and when I woke up, all I saw was the ground heading straight at me. I never saw anything coming up so fast and there was nothing between me and that ground." He stopped and wiped the perspiration from his brow with his sleeve. "I thought for sure I was one dead man, and I just lost it."

I realized that it must have been a most frightening experience to wake up, and see nothing but the earth coming straight at you.

My kid brother Bud would drop in on us through the years. Although he didn't look like me when we were younger, we grew more alike as we grew into men. A lot of people noticed the resemblance at first glance.

Bud, who was a Lieutenant and a paratrooper in the Army, was shot in the liver during the war. In the beginning, his behavior was merely considered odd, but as he started to drink, it continued to worsen. He kept no records. His retirement check was directly deposited in the bank, but sometimes he forgot about it. He'd purchase expensive items, like jewelry and write bad checks. Dad came to the rescue many times and paid off his debts.

JOHN BRAUCHT

Initially we could not put our finger on what was wrong with Bud, but later he was diagnosed with schizophrenia, a psychosis identified by bizarre and delusional behavior, with intellectual and emotional deterioration.

Bud was a wanderer, and spent much time with a doctor in San Antonio who treated him for his problem. There were times he was normal, and sometimes when he knew he was out of control, he'd check himself into the VA.

A LIFETIME WORTH REMEMBERING

"JUNE 25, 1950 TROOPS FROM NORTH KOREA INVADE SOUTH KOREA, PRECIPITATING U.N. INTERVENTION THAT BECOMES KNOWN AS THE KOREAN WAR—IN 1952 JONAS E. SALK DEVELOPS THE FIRST VACCINE AGAINST POLIO"

Chapter Twenty-Seven
1950

The Korean War descended upon us on June 25TH. I received orders from Washington to report to Okinawa by way of San Francisco in a month. My assignment for the next two years was Chief Air Traffic Control Officer.

We decided to visit my parents in Shreveport before I reported for duty. The military packed all our furniture and put it in storage.

Lue and Mom went to my parent's cabin in Hot Springs, while Dad and I stayed in Shreveport with the boys. We wanted to give Lue a little vacation to reap the benefits of the healing Hot Spring waters.

Gene and Ricky came down with the mumps. After they were well, we picked up Lue and Mom, and brought them back to Shreveport.

I took off for California, and Lue and the boys stayed on with my parents. While passing through Texas, the glands around my throat started to hurt and I stopped off at the hospital at Fort Worth.

"I think I have the mumps," I said to the doctor on duty.

He examined my neck and glands. "I don't see any indication of the mumps."

"Doesn't it feel swollen there?" I asked.

He touched my neck again. "No, I don't feel anything unusual."

I felt relieved. "That's great. I'm supposed to be reporting for duty in three days."

"Where are you heading?" he asked.

"The West Coast," I answered.

"Then as Horace Greeley once said, 'go west young man, go west'. You're fine. You might be coming down with a sore throat. Take a couple of aspirin and drink a lot of orange juice."

I took off and was driving into Lubbock, when the pain in my glands got so bad, I decided to stop at Reece Air Force Base hospital.

If I didn't catch the mumps from the boys, I must have had one bad sore throat. I entered the hospital and stopped by the nurse's station.

"I need to see a doctor," I whispered.

A young nurse looked up at me. "What seems to be wrong with you?"

"I think I have the mumps," I replied.

She stood up and backed away. "I haven't had the mumps yet, so I don't want to get near you." She pointed down the hallway. "Just go down there, and go into the first room on the left."

A LIFETIME WORTH REMEMBERING

A doctor examined my glands, which by now were quite swollen. "You have one full blown case of the mumps, young man. We're going to have to check you in for a stay." "But I have to get to 'Frisco', Doctor," I protested. "I'm supposed to be on a boat going to Japan. Can't you just give me a shot or something?"

"Captain, the only place you're going now is to bed. You are highly contagious."

I called Washington and notified them that I was in the hospital and I'd get there as soon as possible.

After seven days, the swelling disappeared and I was feeling fine. The doctor discharged me and I was on my way.

I immediately reported to Transportation Headquarters when I got to San Francisco and was assigned the position of Mess Officer, and within a few days was aboard a small ship heading for Japan.

We arrived in Tokyo, and were housed in the headquarters of an electric company that the United States had converted into a hotel. After a twenty-five cent haircut, my buddy and I took off for a tour through the city.

I was just about to buy earrings and an ivory bracelet for Lue, when my buddy clued me in that I was supposed to bargain. I never liked to haggle over the cost of anything, but he insisted the vendors jacked up the price and expected to bargain. I took his advice and got the jewelry for almost half the original asking price.

After a short stay in Tokyo, I was on my way to Okinawa, the largest of the Ryukyu Islands in the North Pacific, which was taken over by U.S. forces in 1945. The main control

JOHN BRAUCHT

airport was in Naha and the tower and radar approach was at Kadina Air Force Base, where I was stationed.

The base had its own barracks, mess hall, communications center and headquarters. In addition to my rank as Chief Air Traffic Control Officer, I was also in charge of the BX and its activity.

The first project I implemented was a craft activity class. Although women were not allowed to live in that area, a female civilian instructor was hired to teach arts and crafts to the service men. I took advantage of the class and made Lue a beautiful hand tooled leather purse.

After the arts and crafts class was established, I made arrangements to open up a library.

Once the library was set in motion, my next project was building an enclosure for the outdoor theater. When it rained, the men had to sit in the open, wearing their ponchos if they wanted to watch a movie. I made a proposal to build the enclosure, but it was rejected because they didn't have the manpower or materials to build one.

The men heard about the proposal and were disappointed when it was turned down. They enjoyed watching the American movies but didn't relish having to do it in the rain.

I made up my mind to find a way to enclose the theater. I had watched the sitcom, "Sergeant Bilko" many times on television and Bilko always managed to find a way to get things done. And if he could, so could I.

Driving around the base and scouting behind every building, I came across a storage area filled with construction materials. I got out of the car and approached the soldier standing duty by the gate.

A LIFETIME WORTH REMEMBERING

"Can I take a look in there, Private?"

"Yes sir," he said, giving me a salute. "Anything I can help you with?"

I spotted a huge pile of corrugated steel sheets. "Yeah. What's the story on that stuff?"

"The only thing I know sir, is that I'm here to see that the natives don't steal it."

"Look," I said, "I'm trying to help you guys and I'm not getting much help from the brass. But I could sure use those," I said, pointing to the steel.

He thought a moment. "What do you want it for?"

"I'm trying to enclose the movie house so you don't get soaked when it rains."

A grin spread across his face. "How much do you want?"

"As much as you can spare."

"Be my guest, sir. Can I help you with anything else?"

I looked around but didn't see anything I could use. "No thanks, but I really appreciate the steel."

He laughed. "Hey, no problem, sir. The more you take, the less I have to protect."

The next morning, I got a few men together and we loaded the steel sheets onto a couple of trucks. Next we needed lumber. We didn't have to look far. Right behind our communication building, just waiting for the taking, lay a pile of telephone poles.

All that was left were the men to build the theater.

Word got around the camp that I was looking for help. The next day, I got a message that the Post Exchange manager wanted to see me.

"I heard you're looking for help," he said.

"I sure am," I responded.

"Well, I know some natives who are always looking for work. What are you going to pay?"

"Nothing," I said apologetically. "We're doing this project without funds."

The manager scratched his head. "How about giving them some building materials in exchange."

"I don't have a problem with that," I said, grateful that he offered a solution. "But do they have any experience?"

"Yeah. They're all construction workers and carpenters. I've known most of them for a couple of years."

The next day a small group of men arrived at the construction site, ready and anxious for work. I explained what I wanted done, and they started working immediately.

The workers planted the poles deep into the ground to form the framework of the walls. There were no nails, so the joints were set together by tongue and groove and the corrugated walls and roof were held together by thick cables.

Within a few weeks the theater was ready to open. All we lacked was a name. I suggested that we hold a contest. The men could submit a name, and the winner would receive a prize of free candy and popcorn at the theater for the next year.

A Captain, who had been a prisoner in World War II, won with the name 'CEAGUS', which translated means, 'come early and get a seat'.

The theater project was a huge success, much to the surprise of the people who rejected my proposal.

A LIFETIME WORTH REMEMBERING

During one particular rainy period, my fingers began to hurt when I performed even the simplest of chores. They stiffened and swelled at the joints and it was almost impossible to write or type, which was one of my duties. Finally, I had no choice but to see the doctor.

"I suspect you have arthritis in both your hands," he said, after an examination.

"What can I do about it?" I asked.

He shook his head. "Not much, Captain. The best I can do is recommend aspirin."

I tried the aspirin, but it didn't seem to help. I saw the doctor again, and he prescribed 'gold' tablets. The gold didn't help. I tried various treatments for the remaining time I was in Okinawa, but nothing worked. Eventually, I accepted the fact that I would have to live with pain.

After completing the entertainment aspect of my job, I was able to direct my full attention to Air Traffic. Although the United States controlled all traffic between Korea, Japan, Iwo Jima, Guam, Taiwan (Formosa), the Philippines and Hong Kong, all countries were expected to work together.

I became aware that there was a problem with minimum altitude requirements and brought the issue up at a meeting.

"I'd like to point out that the altitude we are using at the southern tip of Taiwan is too low if a plane drifts a little off course," I said, indicating the area on a map. "And that pilot stands a good chance of colliding with that mountain. We are very fortunate that someone hasn't been killed before."

"So, you're suggesting that we raise minimum altitude requirements in the southern tip. Is that correct?" the chief controller from Taiwan asked.

"Absolutely," I responded. "I've studied the situation very carefully."

"Then how do we get this approved?" the Hong Kong controller asked.

"For now," I instructed. "I suggest we instruct all pilots of the new minimum altitude, and I'll make a request that the Air Force make the changes in their new flight charts and maps."

"I would like to request that United States train our men for every aspect of air control," the Taiwan controller suggested.

"I think that we can do that, Captain," I said. "I'll send the personnel over to train your people."

I followed through with the changes, and as a result, our men in Okinawa were sent to Taiwan to assist in their training programs.

We no doubt saved countless lives in locating and guiding aircraft to safety. One British pilot, flying a passenger plane with most of its instruments out of order, was brought to safety because of our work and radar. It was considered quite an endeavor, considering that during the 1950's, we did not have the sophisticated equipment we have today.

The pilot later sent us a clipping from a British newspaper, giving us credit for saving his life. He was thoughtful enough to name me as controller.

When the B-29's took off from Okinawa to bomb Korea, their unit was in control of outgoing aircraft. When the planes returned to base, I was the only controller working at that time. Because of the heavy load of responsibility and pressure I was under, I requested assistance. They sent me a few experienced men but one of them, a Sergeant, did not qualify for top secret clearance.

I checked with personnel and protested their decision.

"Why didn't he pass clearance?" I inquired.

"Because he has a record."

"What did he do?"

"From what the report states, he stole a tire from a filling station when he was a teenager."

When I questioned the Sergeant about the incident, he made it sound like it wasn't anything serious.

"Ah, we were just fooling around with the stuff," he said. "It was a stupid thing to do but I was only a kid then."

I tried to get the decision reversed, but was unable to. If only we realize that the mistakes we make can sometimes come back to haunt us, we'd think twice before committing a crime.

When I arrived in Okinawa, I was not allowed to have my family with me, but after a year and a half, the ruling changed. I immediately wrote Lue, and with the help of the United States government, we made arrangements for her and my sons to be with me. In addition, I was allowed to have our car shipped to Okinawa.

The only drawback was that if I chose to have my family with me, I would have to put in another year there. It wasn't a difficult decision to make.

Lue, Gene and Ricky got all the necessary shots to make the trip to Okinawa. They took a train from Pennsylvania to

San Francisco and from there, sailed to Japan.

Lue had never traveled alone before and she was apprehensive about sailing half way around the world with the boys, but her anxiety to see me overcame any fears she had.

It was almost two years since I had seen my family and I couldn't wait for them to arrive. I flew to Nagasaki and met them at the dock. The boys broke away from Lue when they spotted me and ran into my arms. I was amazed at how big they had grown. Lue looked as beautiful as ever, and her sweet smile that I fell in love with, warmed my heart. It would be wonderful being a family again.

Our house on the base was new and modern, much like houses in the States, though most of the furniture was made of bamboo. Two young girls, Syoko and Tyoko, retained by the government to work for us, received the menial pay of about nine dollars a month but didn't seem to mind the low wages.

Although they were trained to do housework, they did not know how to cook American food. Lue taught the older girl, Tyoko to prepare meals that we were familiar with, while Syoko did most of the housekeeping.

The girls never complained and were under the impression that they couldn't stop working until the work was done. If we didn't tell them to go to bed, they would work throughout the night.

Although we provided them with room and board, Syoko and Tyoko took turns going home on the weekends. That way one of them would always be at the house. The girls smiled all the time and were most obliging and pleasant to have around the house.

A LIFETIME WORTH REMEMBERING

They pampered the boys. Tyoko, who wasn't much bigger than Ricky, waited on them hand and foot, almost to the point of spoiling them.

Ricky was playing outside the house one day when Lue called him in for dinner.

"I want Tyoko to carry me in!" he demanded.

Lue quickly put a stop to that.

JOHN BRAUCHT

A LIFETIME WORTH REMEMBERING

"IN 1953, JOHN GIBBON JR. USES HIS HEART-LUNG MACHINE FOR THE FIRST TIME DURING SURGERY ON A HUMAN BEING—IN 1956, MOVIE QUEEN GRACE KELLY MARRIES PRINCE RAINIER III OF MONACO"

Chapter Twenty-Eight
1953

The three-year hitch was up in Okinawa and Lue and I and the boys were looking forward to returning to the states. When we arrived in San Francisco, one of the first things we did was to buy a car, since we had sold the car we took to Okinawa. Then we took a few days off to tour the sights in our spanking-new Plymouth station wagon.

In the meantime, I learned my next assignment was to be in Springfield, Massachusetts.

With Lue and the boys packed in the wagon, we drove thirty-five hundred miles straight across the United States. It took us about a week to get there, and we stayed in a motel until I was able to find an apartment.

For years we were pretty much used to packing up and moving, but with two small children, it became more difficult and disruptive to their lives. It was not easy for the boys always having to leave their friends behind and adjust to a new school. But they understood that my job was important, and that the moving was part of the job.

After we settled in the apartment, we decided to go to church but didn't know where the closest one was.

I stopped a man walking along the street, and said, "Pardon me sir, but could you please give me directions to the closest Baptist church?"

He pointed north and said, "Go down PahkAH Street, then take your second left and it's about a half mile furthAH down the road."

I wasn't quite sure what he said, so I asked again, "Go down where?"

He looked at me with an odd expression on his face. "I said go down PahkAH."

I scratched my head. "Could you please repeat that again, sir?"

"I said PahkAH, PahkAH! Are you deaf?"

Lue nudged me. "I think the man is trying to say, ParkER, honey."

"Oh, I'm sorry, I thought you said PahkAH."

"That's what I've been telling you," he said. "Don't you understand English?"

All military trained Air Traffic Controllers were required to take a course at a civilian air traffic school in Oklahoma City. I was one of three officers selected for this assignment. I flew out to Oklahoma, and after six weeks of tedious training, I completed the course and was certified as an Air Traffic Controller.

A LIFETIME WORTH REMEMBERING

When I returned to Springfield, I was in for a shock. The Air Force was overstocked with the ranks of First Lieutenants through Majors and had recently issued orders to release thousands of officers.

I was one of them.

JOHN BRAUCHT

"THE U.S. SUPREME COURT RULES AGAINST SCHOOL SEGREGATION BY RACE"

Chapter Twenty-Nine
1954

I only had eighteen years of service and I needed twenty to be eligible to retire with a pension, so after my 'forced discharge', I intended to re-enlist. My first attempt was to seek a position as a helicopter pilot with the Marines with the rank of a Flight Officer.

"You are aware that you'll have to give up your retirement rank as Major if you join the Marines," the recruiter informed me.

After listening to what he had to say, it appeared that a demotion was the only drawback. It was a difficult decision to make, and after weighing all options, I made up my mind to re-enlist in the Air Force Traffic Control Field, the same field I held as an officer.

"The highest rank we can offer you, is a Three Stripe Buck Sergeant," I was told.

I wanted the same position I held at Maxwell so I called Colonel Loomis at Patterson Field in Dayton.

"Colonel Loomis, my name is John Braucht, and I was just riffed from the Air Force."

"What can I do for you, Mr. Braucht?"

"Well, sir," I said, "I'm looking for a position where I have the most experience, and wanted to check with your office first."

"What kind of experience do you have?"

"I was with the AACS at Maxwell, and was Chief Air Traffic Control Officer in Okinawa."

"Actually you called at the right time. I'm looking for experienced controllers," Colonel Loomis said. "And from the sound of it, you certainly are more than qualified. How soon can you make it to Dayton?"

"I'm on my way, sir," I said.

By now we had moved about thirty times. Lue was wonderful, always understanding, never complaining. I suspected that she liked seeing new places and meeting new people, though it must have been very difficult for her. It seemed that just as we were about settled, we'd be uprooted again and heading for a new adventure in another part of the world.

We moved into the Page Manor apartment complex directly across the street from Wright Field.

The first thing we did after getting the place in order was to buy a television and a Pomeranian puppy.

Unfortunately, the puppy got out one day, ran into the street and was hit by a car. We buried him while Gene, who had been taking trumpet lessons, played taps. Lue missed

A LIFETIME WORTH REMEMBERING

the Pomeranian so much we bought a Weimaraner puppy who soon outgrew the apartment, but without a fenced-in back yard, there was no choice but to return him to the people we bought him from.

Lue decided that we shouldn't have another dog at this point in our lives, so we decided on something that was small enough and couldn't escape the apartment. Our choice was a parakeet that we called Petey.

Petey became quite the affectionate pet. When I took a nap on the sofa, he would perch on my chest and nap with me. We were impressed with his intelligence but we misjudged his ability to escape. One day, Lue let him out of his cage and when I walked in the house...Petey flew out. I followed him around the neighborhood and could hardly believe it when he flew toward me and landed on my shoulder.

After that experience, we were always careful not to open the door when the bird was out of the cage.

Even though I took a drastic cut in pay, I was eager and determined to get in the two years necessary for my full retirement.

The job at Patterson Field was not difficult. I typed up reports on all aircraft locations and posted the locations on a board for eight hours a day.

I had been diagnosed with arthritis while I was in Okinawa. When I first started typing, the pain in my fingers was severe, but the more typing I did, the more exercise my fingers got; and the more exercise my fingers got, the more the pain disappeared.

Everything was fine until my right arm began to swell. Although I suspected arthritis, I had it checked out in the base hospital.

"Take a couple of aspirin," the doctor said.

The aspirin did not help and by now my arm hurt so badly that I had to put it in a sling. This turned out to be not such a good idea. Though the sling reduced the pain, my arm started locking up to the point where I couldn't bend it.

One night I was lying on the sofa watching television with Lue sitting on the floor beside me. Just her breath on my arm caused me to scream.

"What's wrong?" she said, backing away.

"You're breathing on my arm!" I yelled.

"You mean just my breathing on you hurts?"

I nodded. "It makes it worse if possible."

She kissed me on the forehead. "Honey, you have to see the doctor tomorrow morning. You can't go on like this."

The next day I went back to the Infirmary and was examined by Doctor Taylor, who was new on the staff.

"You've got a severe case of rheumatoid arthritis," he said. "What have you been doing for it?"

"I tried a lot of things, Doctor, from aspirin to gold. Nothing works."

He took out his prescription pad and started writing. "To begin with, take two of these each day after meals."

"What is it?" I asked, as he handed me the prescription.

"*Butazolodene*. It should help the pain and the swelling. And get rid of that sling."

I took the pills as he prescribed and in a few days the swelling went down. When the pain subsided, I stopped

A LIFETIME WORTH REMEMBERING

taking the pills.

Just when I thought my arthritis was cured, my right hip began giving me trouble. I went back to the hospital and saw the specialist on duty.

"I think we better try *Cortisone*," he said. "I'll have to give you an injection straight into the hip. Hopefully this will do the trick."

It didn't. After leaving the hospital, I went to my office and tried to work but the pain became unbearable. Two of my friends had to carry me to my car and drive me to the hospital.

After I was given a shot of morphine, my friends drove me home and put me to bed. The morphine did little to alleviate the pain and it grew increasingly worse. I tossed and moaned throughout the night.

"Is there anything I can do?" Lue would ask.

There was nothing she could do and by this time, I was doubtful that the doctors could do anything either. Early the next morning, I went back to see the specialist.

"I'll give you another shot of Cortisone," he said.

"No sir," I replied, remembering the results of the last shot. "I think your cure is worse than my ailment."

He laughed, and sat down at his desk. "Then, Doctor Braucht, what would you suggest we do?"

I thought for a moment then told him, "I saw Doctor Taylor for the arthritis in my arm a while ago, and he gave me some pills called Butazolodene."

"Did they help?"

"Yes, very much so."

He took out his prescription pad. "Do you have any left

or do you need more?"

"I've got about half a bottle left."

"Take three a day until they're gone," he said, putting the pad away. "Then come back if you need more and I'll write you out a new prescription."

I followed the specialist's instructions until the last of the pills were gone. The pain miraculously disappeared and I never experienced an attack like that again.

Most of the men I worked with, who had ten or more years in Air Traffic Control, experienced problems with their hearts, ulcers and nerves, and many were addicted to drugs.

Many of these illnesses were attributed to the tension they were faced with every day. The responsibility of passengers and crew safety has proven that Air Traffic Control is one of the most stressful jobs in existence.

A LIFETIME WORTH REMEMBERING

"NARINDER KAPARY OF LONDON PRODUCES THE FIRST OPTICAL FIBERS"

Chapter Thirty
1955

Our neighbor, Jack Humphries, who was a captain in the Air Force, wanted to have a church on the east side of town as well as the one on the west side. Many of the families had no transportation and it was difficult for them to attend services because the west side church was so far away.

Captain Jack and his wife, Mildred, held a meeting in his apartment. Lue and I, Mr. & Mrs. Grubbs, Colonel & Mrs. Givens and Mr. & Mrs. Babbs decided to form our own church. After electing the officers and deacons, we hired a fine young preacher, twenty-three year old, Orville Griffin.

Our next move was to rent the Lawton School to hold services.

Pastor Griffin worked with the original families in the early life of the mission, which would later become the East Dayton Baptist Church.

During the period of working with the church committees,

which took a lot of my time, I was only receiving an extra fifty-percent of base pay as a pilot. Now that I was an enlisted Sergeant, there was a big drop in my income and it wasn't enough to support my family without dipping into our saving resources.

Lue and I decided to go into business. We investigated Blairs, a well-known cosmetic distributor, and liked what we found. I became the sales representative for the state of Ohio selling wholesale cosmetics, while Lue kept records. Sales did so well, that we were able to hire distributors to do the work for us.

Having a sales staff gave me the time to go into the furniture and appliance field. It was a lucrative field, and one that I was quite familiar with because of my previous experience in Shreveport.

After locating a building in a good downtown location, I began dealing with the wholesalers who would supply the furniture and appliances on assignment. I hired some help and named the business Bilkos, after Sergeant Bilko who always found a way to get things done.

Gene, now a teenager, had a natural talent for mimicry and loved to listen to the weather reports on the radio. Lue occasionally brought the boys to spend the day with me at Bilkos.

Gene quickly learned how to use an old recorder, and would talk into the microphone for hours.

"You be the weatherman," he told Ricky, "and I'll be the newsman."

"Okay," Ricky said.

A LIFETIME WORTH REMEMBERING

Gene, altering his voice, spoke into the microphone. "And that's it for today's news, ladies and gentlemen. And now we'll hear from the weather man." He handed the microphone to Ricky.

Ricky cleared his throat. "The weather today will be clear and cloudy with 'shattered' showers."

Every time we remember what he said, we have a good chuckle. Ricky isn't as amused as the rest of the family.

I worked three straight days at Patterson and was off two. This gave me enough time to get the business started and train the help.

Lue took care of the house, the boys, and kept the books for both businesses. Everything was working out fine so it didn't take long for me to go into still another business.

This one however, would be a gamble. It was a field I was not familiar with but it was a field that I recognized had potential.

I borrowed ten-thousand dollars from my life insurance policies and bought ten acres of cornfields. According to the law, the corn as well as the property now belonged to me but the seller was under the impression that the corn belonged to him. When the corn was ready for harvest, much to his disappointment, he discovered he had no legal claim to any profit.

I felt sorry for him and decided to split the profits fifty fifty.

After the corn was sold, I had the land surveyed, put in roads, and divided it into eighteen half-acre lots. Then I got with Bob Lang, a builder, whose son was the junior choir director at the church. We drew up a contract, went to the bank, and I signed a construction loan to build houses on the property. This risky enterprise turned out to be the easiest and most profitable one I ever engaged in.

    The most difficult thing I had to do was sign my name a half-dozen times.

Bob built us a dream house on one of the sites, with a half-acre left to raise a garden. This was the home we intended to live in after retirement.

    Gene, now 14, had been selling gladiolus and decided he could make more profit if he grew and sold his own. He purchased gladiola bulbs with his savings, and within the year harvested a healthy crop.

    In addition to his flower business, Gene decided to become a paperboy. We helped him get the afternoon paper route. Lue helped him while he was in school. She rolled up the newspapers and bound them together with rubber bands.

    "You push," Gene told Ricky, after they had loaded their wagon with papers. "And I'll pull."

    They had no sooner turned the corner than Ricky leaned on the wagon and tipped it over.

    "You're supposed to help, not cause problems!" Gene yelled, as he started picking up the papers.

    Ricky looked like he was going to cry.

    "But, I guess it was only an accident and no harm done."

    Ricky grinned. "I won't do it again."

Even though Gene and Ricky kept busy taking golf, swimming and tennis lessons, they were always looking for ways to make money. "Chips off the old block if you ask me," Lue would say.

She took them strawberry picking at a neighbor's farm. Every time she filled a basket, the boys would take it and replace it with an empty one. At the end of the day, they had picked about eighty quarts of berries and the boys had eaten about a quart apiece.

"I'm going to join the FBI when I get older," Gene informed us one evening.

Our Pastor, who was visiting us at the time, thought it prudent to offer Gene advice. "It's a dangerous profession, Gene. Are you sure you want such a job?"

"Yes," Gene said, undaunted by the Pastor's remarks.

"You'll be dealing with murderers and thieves and kidnappers. Your life will be on the line all the time."

"I don't care," Gene said with conviction. "It's what I want to do."

Lue and I didn't bring up the subject again. We hoped Gene would forget about the FBI and select a less perilous career, if we didn't oppose him.

In addition to all our other endeavors, Lue and I were kept busy in the church. On Sundays, she played the piano and sang specials in the choir, while I welcomed members to the service and helped out in the children's nursery. I was Chairman of the Board of Deacons, the Bond Drive and the Building Committee.

JOHN BRAUCHT

A LIFETIME WORTH REMEMBERING

"ALASKA BECOMES THE 49TH STATE AND HAWAII BECOMES THE 50TH STATE"

Chapter Thirty-One
1959

The winter of 1959 was the coldest Dayton had seen in years and Lue and I did not look forward to spending another frigid winter there. My arthritis was acting up and I had trouble walking and standing.

I woke up one morning and looked out the window. It was snowing and the wind was howling. The weather report warned: "Prepare for a blizzard".

"Hey, honey," I said, winking at Lue. "I just heard we've been transferred to California."

She laughed. "We can't be transferred. We're not in the service anymore."

"Well, I figured I'd get your full attention if I said that."

"And you did. So John, where do we want to live in California?"

"Anywhere the snow doesn't fall," I said jokingly.

I went to the library, found some books on California

and started doing some research. We had lived there in the past and loved it, but this would probably be our last move so it was important to make the right choice.

We had second thoughts about California after we learned about the problems it was having with smog, the sharp increase in crime, and the high cost of living.

"Let's look at Florida," I said. "California isn't as attractive as it used to be."

Lue nodded. "And I hear the climate's better, and it's a lot cheaper too."

We contacted the St. Petersburg Chamber of Commerce who was happy to supply us with brochures of their city and was given a very bright picture. According to statistics, job opportunities in the furniture and insurance business were plentiful; cost of living was one of the lowest in the nation; smog was non-existent, and they boasted 360 days of sunshine.

"I think we're going to be transferred to St. Petersburg, Florida," I said.

Lue grinned, "Florida, here we come."

I found a buyer for the furniture store, closed out the Blair cosmetic's accounts and resigned from Church committees and the Board of Directors. I sought legal advice and gave power of attorney to Bob Lang, the contractor to complete the land development project to build houses and to send me my share of the profits as agreed upon.

In July, we made arrangements to have our furniture put in storage until we found a permanent residence in Florida. My parents were visiting us at the time and talked

A LIFETIME WORTH REMEMBERING

us into spending a couple of weeks at their cabin in Hot Springs before we moved to Florida. We agreed, but first Lue and I wanted to take a few days off in Canada. Ricky didn't want to go with us, so he went to the cabin with Mom and Dad and Gene went along with us on our second honeymoon in Niagara Falls.

We crossed into Canada and got a room at a hotel with a view of the falls. We ate dinner that evening on a roof top restaurant that over looked the falls. At night, brightly colored spotlights illuminated the cascading water and mist, making it a most spectacular sight.

As we looked over the menu, Gene was quick to comment, "Four dollars for a dinner. We can't afford that, Dad."

"Well, I think we can this time," I said. "So enjoy it."

"Besides," Lue added, "the scenery is worth it."

In addition to exploring the falls from all angles, and a boat ride to the base of the falls, we decided to walk under them. We donned yellow slickers, which protected us from the constant heavy spray. It was an awesome experience.

We spent the next few days sightseeing and to Gene's delight, he discovered firecrackers in a souvenir shop. He made a large selection and was heading for the cashier when I stopped him.

"I don't think you ought to buy those," I said.

"But I want them Dad," he whined.

"I'm almost positive that they're illegal in the states," I added.

"No they're not," he argued. "And besides it's my own money."

I decided to let him learn a lesson the hard way, and

when we stopped at the U.S. immigration station, we were asked to identify any purchases made in Canada.

I had no choice but to be honest, and produced all the things we had bought. Gene reluctantly showed them the firecrackers and was heartbroken when they confiscated his purchases. He not only lost the firecrackers but lost his hard-earned money as well.

We stopped at Dayton to pick up some personal belongings and our *Volkswagen* company truck. After saying goodbye to our friends, it was agreed that Lue and Gene would drive the station wagon to Hot Springs and stay with my parents until I found a house in St. Petersburg.

They took off for Hot Springs, and I loaded up the Volkswagen with all our personal belongings and took off for Florida.

The sun was shining and the temperature hovered in the high 80's when I arrived in St. Petersburg. Fortunately, Lue's aunt Bertha and uncle Fred lived there in a two-bedroom trailer in a mobile park. I stayed with them until I checked out the areas that Lue and I wanted to live in.

Finally, I located a subdivision of new homes in Holiday Park. I toured several of the model homes, and settled on a three-bedroom house in a location that seemed perfect for our needs.

The house I chose was in the middle of a curve. With a large back yard that bordered on a pretty little creek, it seemed perfect for raising children...even a dog if we so decided.

After calling Lue, and telling her about the house, I had

A LIFETIME WORTH REMEMBERING

the furniture shipped from Dayton. As soon as the movers carried it in the house, I was at McDill Air Force Base hopping a ride to Little Rock. Dad picked me up at the airport and we drove to Hot Springs.

Before we left for Florida, Dad wanted to take us for a ride on his motor boat. Mom packed a lunch and Dad piled Ricky, Gene and me into his boat and we motored up the lake to a dam.

It was well after one o'clock when we docked the boat. Everyone was starving and couldn't wait to eat lunch. Ricky and Gene unpacked the boat, while Dad and I gathered kindling to start a fire.

"Bring the franks over here, Ricky," Dad yelled.

Ricky tore into the picnic basket and took out potato salad, pickles and a package of hot dog rolls. "Where are they?" he yelled back.

"In the basket," I said.

"No they're not!" he yelled.

I walked over and looked in the basket. "They should be in here," I said, double-checking. "But they're not."

"Well, Dad," Ricky said. "We can always roast the pickles instead."

We had a laugh and realized that Mom forgot the franks. We filled up on the potato salad, pickles and rolls. At that point anything tasted good.

After lunch, we motored out to the middle of the lake. I tossed the anchor overboard while Dad baited a worm on a hook.

"I think the fish should be pretty hungry right about now," he said.

JOHN BRAUCHT

"But I don't want to fish, Grampa," Ricky said. "I want to go swimming."

"Yeah, we want to go swimming," Gene echoed.

"The water's too cold," Dad said.

"No, Grampa. We don't care," Gene argued.

"The water's not cold at the cabin," Ricky whined.

"Let them find out for themselves, Dad," I intervened. "Besides, I want to fish."

Dad shook his head. "Okay boys, have it your way but don't swim too far from the boat and don't say we didn't warn you."

Dad and I cast our lines away from the boys, just as they dove off the boat. In seconds they were clamoring to get back in the boat.

"It's freezing!" they screamed. "We wanna get back in the boat!"

Dad and I looked at each other and laughed as we helped them climb back in.

"Now will you believe me when I tell you something," Grandpa said.

I reached for a couple of towels and wrapped them around their shoulders.

"Yesss, Grandpa," Ricky managed to say through chattering teeth.

By now all the screaming and fuss had driven the fish away so we called it a day and headed back to the cabin with two shivering but wiser boys.

We spent a few more days with the family before taking off for our new home in Florida. I had described the house to Lue, and she was anxious to see it.

A LIFETIME WORTH REMEMBERING

When we drove down the palm-lined street of single family homes in St. Petersburg, and pulled into our driveway, Lue's eyes lit up. A beautiful smile spread across her face and I knew I had chosen the perfect house.

Lue was first out of the car, with the boys and me after her. After inspecting all the rooms, and all the closets, Lue turned to me. "I love it, John," she said. "It's perfect. You did a wonderful job."

"Yeah, Dad," Gene said. "I got my own room picked out."

"Me too," Ricky screamed. "I want the one in the back."

I was relieved that everyone was pleased with the house. We took a tour around the neighborhood and discovered a nearby pasture with grazing horses that reminded us of the farm. There were a lot of young children in the area, and the boys immediately made friends.

Lue was delighted to finally have a home where she could plant things in the ground and see them grow. We went to Earl's Nursery, and loaded up on fruit trees, bushes and flowering plants.

She wanted to try her hands with orchids and bought an 'Alice Pierce', a cattleya white orchid with a purple throat. With her loving care and a green thumb, the orchid flourished. Her interest in orchids grew to the point where we had almost five-thousand orchids. The original plant grew so large it had over seventy blooms at one time.

We gave cuttings away to our local neighbors and friends around the United States. Some were even sold to florists. Many of the orchids that we sold, won prizes in flower shows.

In later years, Lue's health made it impossible to give

the orchids the lavish attention they needed, and my work took up all my spare time, so we passed the word along that the orchids were for sale and they were immediately sold.

September rolled around and it was time to enroll the boys in school. Gene was now a sophomore in High School and Ricky, who still took his 'teddy bear' to bed with him, was in the fifth grade.

It wasn't long before I felt restless and started looking for something to do. I took a temporary job setting up the appliance department with a new *Grand Union* store just for something to do and was paid well for my services.

"AMERICA LAUNCHES THE WEATHER SATELLITE, TIROS 1"

Chapter Thirty-Two
1960

I applied for a job at the U.S. Post Office and passed their exam with a good grade. Starting with a sitting position in mail routing, I then received a promotion to deliver the mail. This meant a lot of walking. Initially it did my arthritis a lot of good, even more so when I had a bicycle route.

One morning after sorting the mail, I started over to pick up my delivery bag. My joints were so stiff, that I was walking with a limp.

"What's wrong with you?" my supervisor asked. "Why are you walking like that?"

I had no choice but to tell him the truth. "I've got arthritis."

He shook his head. "Why didn't you let us know when you applied for this job?"

"I thought I had it under control, but I guess I didn't after all."

JOHN BRAUCHT

"I'm sorry John, but I have no alternative but to let you go."

At first I thought of contesting his decision to fire me, but I realized that my health wouldn't permit me to work delivery, and the only other positions would be either standing or sitting, and neither one was good for my hip.

After my family and I settled into a routine life, I started to exercise on a routine basis and read several books about arthritis; the New England Folk Medicine, and a book by Art Linkletter and his mother's arthritis.

"When my mother would walk, she squeaked," Linkletter said.

I was surprised to learn that if you drank cold water with your meals, the fat in your system would congeal and not be digested. This did not help people afflicted with arthritis, as they need the fat to keep the joints lubricated.

Following the sensible advice in the books, and in addition to my exercising, the pain in my joints began to disappear.

I received a notice from the military to report to the hospital in Maxwell Air Force Base for a final determination of my retirement status.

I hopped a plane out of McDill and arrived at the hospital where they checked out the condition of my arthritis. The diagnosis was that I had improved. They decreased my disability from fifty percent to ten percent.

A LIFETIME WORTH REMEMBERING

In September, the Permanent Retirement recommended a disability of ten percent but turned around and suggested that I contest the recommendation. I did as they suggested, and surprisingly was awarded a permanent twenty percent disability.

A month later, I received a call from Joe Gibson, a representative of *Prudential Insurance Company* who wanted to meet me, and invited him over to the house.

He explained that Mom had told him I would make a good salesman for Prudential and was interested in my coming to work for the company.

A second meeting took place in Tampa, where the Area Manager of fourteen counties and Fred Durance, his assistant, interviewed me. I told them about my previous experience in the insurance field, and was hired on the spot. After a short training period, I was put on allowance pay that started me out at ninety dollars a week. This starting pay would decrease every thirteen weeks, until I was on straight commission.

By the end of the thirteen weeks, my commissions were averaging four-hundred dollars a week.

When the company divided the fourteen counties into seven, Fred was put in charge of the West Coast of Florida.

"You know John," he said, "when I first met you, I didn't think you'd work out. The coach and Joe voted for you but I had reservations."

"What do you mean?" I asked.

"You didn't brag about yourself."

"I'm not quite sure what you mean, Fred."

"I mean that I thought that you wouldn't be able to use the hard sell."

Maybe I was too soft, I thought. I never wanted to sell anything to anyone who didn't need it. I believed that repeat sales proved that people trusted you. "That depended on how you look at it, Fred," I said. "It's not what you say about yourself that counts, but what you can achieve in life that counts. If a person has no proof of accomplishment or doesn't have a record to show what he has done in life then he has no right to brag."

"That's true," he agreed. "Anyway, I sure misjudged you. And you taught me to judge people by their accomplishments."

When Grampa Melvin and Grampa Kay Messinger followed us to Florida in 1961, Grampa Melvin got me involved with the Kiwanis Club. It was at that time that I became a good friend with the postmaster.

"I worked for the Post Office for a short time," I told him one day.

"Why did you leave?" he asked.

I proceeded to tell him what had happened.

"You know, John," he replied, "they had no right to fire you. Since you were stricken with arthritis while you were in the line of duty, you could file a judgment against the Post Office."

"What good would that do me?" I inquired.

"I think you could be reimbursed for all your wages to date. If you want, I'll help you file a claim."

I thought it over for a few seconds, and said, "I do

A LIFETIME WORTH REMEMBERING

appreciate your trying to help me, but I'm doing pretty good with Prudential."

JOHN BRAUCHT

A LIFETIME WORTH REMEMBERING

"IN 1961, ALAN SHEPARD JR. BECOMES THE FIRST U.S. ASTRONAUT IN SPACE WHEN HE COMPLETES A 15 MINUTE SUBORBITAL FLIGHT ON FREEDOM 7"

Chapter Thirty-Three
1961

Most of the time while I was working at Prudential, I was one of the top three salesmen in my unit. I attended most of the conventions, because I either met or exceeded the sales quota set by the President's Club.

Sometimes I was able to take Lue and Ricky with me to the conventions in Montreal, New Orleans, Denver, Washington D.C., the Bahamas and New York City during the World's Fair. My expenses and half of my family's expenses were paid by Prudential and traveling was a wonderful learning experience for the boys.

JOHN BRAUCHT

"A VACCINE AGAINST MEASLES BECOMES AVAILABLE."

Chapter Thirty-Four

By 1965 I was promoted to Division Manager, but was required to build my own division. To do this, I advertised for experienced insurance salesmen, hired a staff and trained them in our particular type of sales. I insisted I would not tolerate any misrepresentation or dishonesty of any kind. If they did so, they would be fired on the spot. I instructed them to sell only the amount of insurance a client could afford, and not because of what it would benefit them in commissions.

As a result of this philosophy, my customers trusted me, bought whatever my salesmen suggested and recommended our company to their friends.

I began to advise my customers on how to invest in stocks and bonds, due to my own success in these ventures.

While I was with Prudential, I engaged in a 'side-line' enterprise. I purchased ten candy vending machines and placed them throughout St. Petersburg. I made a deal with a local candy wholesaler to buy the candy for five and six cents a bar, which I placed in the machines and sold for ten cents. Later, I located the companies that made the candy and dealt with them direct. The candy was fresher and cost less.

As my 'side-line' enterprise grew, I continued to buy bigger and better machines, and placed them in more upscale locations. I met other vendors and made deals to sell them candy at a cheaper price than they had been paying.

Everything was going fine, but it was taking a lot more time to keep up with the growing business, so when two women wanted to buy me out, I named my price and they accepted.

"SOVIET SHIPS BRING GUIDED MISSLES TO CUBA, SETTING OFF THE CUBAN MISSILE CRISIS"

Chapter Thirty-Five
1962

The secretary of the Kiwanis was selling stocks and bonds to build the Metropolitan General hospital in Pinellas Park, Florida. When the hospital was completed, a group of shareholders called a meeting, which I attended. Reports showed that the hospital was operating at a loss, and the shareholders realized that something needed to be done to make it a financially sound institution. A vote was taken to dismiss the builder.

"What we need to do now is elect a new president and administrator," a shareholder suggested.

Another rose from his chair. "I agree. What we need now is for one of us to take over the responsibility of president and administrator, until we can hire the right people for the job."

I volunteered and was unanimously elected president and administrator.

Initially, the hospital had difficulty getting doctors to

refer patients to Metropolitan because of its poor condition, but after most of the problems were resolved and improvements made, the patients started pouring in.

Just about the time that the hospital was showing a profit, the builder called a stockholder's meeting and informed everyone that he and his partner had the controlling stock in Metropolitan.

He had acquired large blocks of shares with the excuse; "I deserved those shares because I got investors to use their money to build the hospital. Instead of taking a 'finder's fee', I chose stocks instead."

His partner, who brought in some of the equipment, said he had also taken shares in lieu of payment.

They brought a group of doctors to the meeting who offered to purchase the hospital for fifty cents on the dollar. This was a surprise to the other shareholders, and most of them decided to accept the same deal.

I felt that my money was safe because I was sure the doctors would make a go of the hospital.

The stockholders called a meeting in to change the hospital policy to one of a non-profit.

The doctors recommended that the shareholders be paid fifty cents on the dollar. Everyone accepted the proposal but I suggested that they should receive what they had paid. The requirement was that all voters must approve, in order to become non-profit. It was decided they must conform to the rules to become non-profit.

A LIFETIME WORTH REMEMBERING

Lue and I joined the Azalea Church when we had moved to St. Petersburg. She played the piano for the children's Sunday school and sang in the choir. I was elected to the deacon board and one of my responsibilities was to teach the Bible to the intermediate group of boys.

One young student, an exceptionally bright boy, was constantly disrupting the class. He made grotesque faces, spoke out of turn, and teased the other kids. Deciding to use a little psychology, I called him aside and said, "You are a very smart young man and the other kids look up to you."

He shrugged. "So?"

"So, you could be a leader if you put your mind to it."

He seemed to ponder what I was saying then said, "How am I supposed to do that, Mr. Braucht?"

"You set the example and they'll follow. When you fool around, they laugh and nobody learns anything. But if you behave, the others will too."

My little pep talk must have done some good because he immediately became a model student.

When the pastor of Azalea left for South America to become a missionary, Lue and I changed over to the Northside church, where we continued to be active.

My responsibility there was to teach a class of ten twelve-year old boys.

At the first meeting, I introduced myself. "My name is John Braucht and I'll be your teacher for the year. I want to teach you how to study. There is only one answer for instance. In math, two times two is always four, just as an original word never contradicts itself. I will give you an assignment to be learned, an assignment that we will be working on for some weeks ahead. The word we'll use is, 'love'. I want you to look it up as many times as you can in the New Testament. This is how you will learn from repetition.

"You mean like we do in school?" a tall boy asked.

"Exactly," I said. "I'll teach you how to remember. Once you learn the technique, like you remember the formulas like you do in math, it will stay in your mind forever."

"Where do we find this word 'love'? In the dictionary?" Another boy asked.

"No, son. We find the word 'love' in a concordance."

"A concordance?" another was quick to inquire. "What's a concordance?"

Good question, young man. The concordance is similar to the dictionary, but it only tells you where to find the word you're looking for in the Bible. It does not, however, like the dictionary, give the definition of the word."

"Where can I get that book?" the same boy asked.

"Your parents should have one, but if they don't they can get one at a Christian Bible bookstore. If your parents can't afford one, I'll be glad to give you one. Once you have the concordance, you will look up the word as many times as you can, and you will never forget it."

The following week, after reading their assignments, we began to discuss them. After doing this for a couple of weeks, we voted on the more outstanding ones that showed them how to show their love for God and others. The boys settled on three and suggested we say them at each meeting.

They are as follows: One, God is love. Two, The fruit of

the spirit is love, joy, peace, patience, gentleness, faithfulness, meekness, and self-control. And, Three, Love is patient and kind. Love is not jealous. Love is not bragging, not puffed up, not indecent, not self seeking, not incensed, not doing evil, not rejoicing in injustice, yet is rejoicing together, is forgoing all, is enduring all.

After class, an assistant pastor stopped by to see me.

"Hello, Mr. Braucht," he said with a smile. "I thought I'd take this opportunity to stop by and tell you what a good job you are doing with the boys. I spoke with several of the parents. They were delighted with what their children were learning, and how it was changing their lives. Some of them suggested you teach a course on *Galatians* to the adults."

"I'd be honored to," I said.

JOHN BRAUCHT

"PRESIDENT JOHN F. KENNEDY IS ASSASSINATED"

Chapter Thirty-Six
1963

Gene graduated from high school and was called for a six-month military duty in South Carolina. He completed the training and returned home, determined to work for the FBI. Nothing the pastor said to him earlier had changed his mind. He did a little research, drove to Jacksonville and passed the requirements without a hitch.

He came home, packed his belongings and was ready to return to Jacksonville for training on the following Monday.

"It would be nice if you went to church with us today," I suggested. "We might not get to see much of you after you leave tomorrow."

"Gee, Dad, I got a chance to go water skiing with the guys," he said.

Gene would later regret his decision. He had an accident while he was water skiing and hurt his knee. When he reported for his physical the next day, they noticed his swollen and bruised knee. He did not meet the physical requirements to enter the academy because of his injury.

After the Messingers followed us to Florida in 1960, Grandma Kay wrote a letter to Mr. Knoch, who made dyes and reproduced the exact letters from the original Greek scripture. She wanted to know if he knew anyone in St. Petersburg who studied the Greek Scriptures. Mr. Knoch immediately replied, and gave us the names of Pastor Earl Brown and his wife, Hazel, their daughter, Ruth Rice and her husband, Marvin and their young daughter, Sandy, who would later become the office manager of our Bible Material business.

Grandma Kay contacted the families and we set up a meeting at Pastor Brown's house to study. The classes grew as word spread, but when Hazel passed away, Pastor Brown could no longer conduct the study groups in his home.

We were able to continue the classes at our house, until Grandpa Melvin passed away in 1976 and Grandma Kay came to live with us. Our children were long gone and the house seemed empty. One of our three bedrooms was converted into an office for the Bible library, and the other was perfect for Grandma Kay.

She was a gifted artist and president of the local art association, and passed away in March of 1997, just four months shy of her one-hundredth birthday.

After Pastor Brown could no longer continue on with the classes, Marvin Rice took over. Classes like this are all over the world. We supplied the Greek text, bibles and related material to churches that were subsequently

A LIFETIME WORTH REMEMBERING

formed as a result of these Greek Scripture classes.

There are also groups that have what we call 'Conferences' or 'Fellowships' around the world.

Gerhard Rutsch, a dear friend and Greek student from California, came to visit us.

"Germany and Switzerland worked together in the Greek Scriptures," he said. "They have more people in attendance than any other country."

I told him that the first Conference our group attended was in Lakeland in 1968 and was headed by Pastor R.Clay Kent from Melbourn, Florida. I started a Conference in St. Petersburg and helped the one in Columbus, Georgia that moved to Waganer, South Carolina under the direction of Pastor Rick Farwell.

There are more Fellowships in Michigan than any other state and members from the United States intermingle with Canada.

One of my greatest joys was to have a young man by the name of Keven Berry come down from Lansing, Michigan to help our work and talk in our classes. Even though he had been in an automobile accident and was crippled and his speech was not perfect, he had a great love for the Lord. He was well versed in the Bible and taught us many things...especially, not to give up. I count him as one of my best friends.

JOHN BRAUCHT

"BEATLEMANIA SWEEPS THE U.S. AS THE ALBUM 'MEET THE BEATLES' SELLS 2 MILLION COPIES"

Chapter Thirty-Seven
1964

Lue's health, which had never been too good, took a turn for the worse and she suffered a heart attack.

A few years earlier, Doctor Swenson operated on a small tumor on her nose. A doctor, who referred Lue to Doctor Swenson, did not inform him that she should not be given certain medications. We learned that the medications Doctor Swenson prescribed subsequently caused her heart attack.

I checked with several doctor friends and the Physician's Association to recommend a specialist for Lue.

We were referred to Doctor Mason, a heart specialist with an excellent reputation. He accepted Lue as his patient, and took care of her until she was well enough to leave the hospital.

But, Lue's heart condition deteriorated and she was in the Intensive Care Unit a total of twenty times in a three year period. To make matters worse, she was also plagued with a bad back and had two back surgeries plus a knee replacement.

While waiting for Lue to have physical therapy for her knee at the rehabilitation center at Bayfront Hospital, I decided to get some exercise myself. I started climbing the stairs. At first I could only make it to the third floor, but before long I was able to climb seven flights of stairs, and worked up to forty times with ease.

Nothing dampened Lue's spirits. In spite of everything she was going through, she would go around the house singing, "Have any rivers you think are uncrossable, have any mountains you can't tunnel through? God specializes in things called impossible, He can do what no one else can do."

She amused herself by doing needlepoint. Her first attempt, which turned out to be a piece of art, was called *The Milk Maid*, a 35 x 29 copy of a French artist's painting, We had it framed and it hangs in our living room today.

Lue decided to try her hand with pettipoint, which was so delicate that she had to use a powerful magnifying glass.

It was not much later, when Lue would discover a new love. One of her cousins came to visit and brought along a collection of pearl buttons. Lue was intrigued with the beauty and diversity of the buttons, and I was amazed at their value.

"Let's go to Ocala," she said to me a few days later. "I need to talk to my cousin again."

I was happy to oblige. "Sure," I said, "But why?"

A LIFETIME WORTH REMEMBERING

"I've decided I want to collect buttons. Antique ones."

The next day we were off to Ocala. It was a pleasant change from the flat terrain of the Tampa Bay Area. Rolling hills and massive oaks, webbed with Spanish moss, provided shade for thousands of purebred cattle and thoroughbred horses.

We purchased a small collection of buttons from her cousin, which was the beginning of a fascinating hobby for Lue. As her collection grew, she joined the Bay Area Button Club, where she was appointed the position of 'Sunshine Lady'. Her responsibility was to send out monthly notices of the meetings, as well as birthday and get well cards. In addition to the selling and bartering of buttons, a new program on buttons is delivered by one of the members at each meeting.

As Lue got more involved in the hobby, I became more curious about their origin.

"What's so interesting about buttons?" I asked Lue one day, as she was organizing a box of rare Chinese buttons.

"Believe it or not, John, they can tell the history of our country." She looked at the Chinese buttons. "And these can tell you about China. Like when they were made, and who wore them."

Each year a State and National Button show is held at a large hotel and people attend from all parts of the world. The members decorate cards with their most interesting and unusual buttons and enter them in the show.

Instructors explain how to decorate the cards for competition and give the latest information about buttons.

JOHN BRAUCHT

"THE WORST NUCLEAR ACCIDENT IN THE U.S. OCCURS AT THE 'THREE MILE ISLAND' NUCLEAR REACTOR"

Chapter Thirty-Eight
1979

After twenty years with Prudential, I called it quits and retired from my second career. I loved to travel, and since I had worked for so many years, I thought it was time to relax and do something just for pleasure. Ricky was away in college and Gene, who was living on his own, worked for *Publix* in the meat department. It was the first time in years that we were alone and gainfully unemployed...with the exception of the Bible business. Now we had time to enjoy life.

I decided to surprise Lue. She was in the kitchen washing the dinner dishes, when I came up beside her, picked up a towel and proceeded to help dry.

"How does a second honeymoon sound to you?" I asked.

She turned to me and grinned. "What are you up to now?"

"Just what I said. A second honeymoon. So what do you say?"

She wiped her hands on her apron, and gave me a kiss.

"I say that sounds wonderful. Where do you want to go?"

"Oh, I don't know," I teased. "Maybe we could start off with dinner at one of your favorite restaurants."

"*Marios!*" she screamed. "Do you mean Marios in Denver?"

I laughed. "Do you know any other Mario?"

She shook her head and said, "No, and it sounds wonderful and romantic. When?"

"How does tomorrow sound?"

She took off her apron and headed for the bedroom. "I'm already packing, honey."

"Pack enough for a couple of weeks. We can swing by Shreveport and say hello to my folks first."

We packed in a hurry and by early morning were on our way to Colorado.

We planned to do some sightseeing as part of our vacation. Our first stop was an egg museum in Vernon, Texas, where the eggs ranged from pea to dinosaur size. From there we went to *Dinosaur Land* where we watched scientists uncovering the remains of prehistoric creatures out of rock with small picks and brushes.

After a quick tour of the Air Force Academy in Colorado, then I suggested crossing over the Royal Gorge. When Lue saw the threatening sway of the suspension bridge hovering over the deep gorge, she stepped back and shook her head.

"There's no way I'm taking one step on that thing."

It was late in the day when we checked into the *Royal Gorge Hotel*, where we had stayed before on several occasions. We were looking forward to dining at Marios, which

A LIFETIME WORTH REMEMBERING

was one of our favorite restaurants. The owner, a well-respected teacher of music, helped many of his proteges to make a successful singing career in opera and in the movies. The food was excellent and the singing waiters added to the atmosphere.

I called for reservations and was disappointed to learn that Marios was closed for renovations so we settled for dinner at the hotel.

At daybreak we took off for the Grand Tetons, then drove the entire range of Yellowstone National Park. The next stop was to the Bad Lands for an afternoon of gemstone mining where the owners 'salt' the area with pellets with semi-precious stones. We were fortunate and struck 'pay dirt". Our next stop was to Mt. Rushmore where our great presidents are carved out of a mountain. This was not only an awesome sight, but an awesome accomplishment.

In addition we took a tour of President Eisenhower's home and were impressed with the gifts he received from famous people throughout the world.

By the time we returned home, I was anxious to get back into a routine. Although I had always been active in *Kiwanis*, *Optimists* and the *Masons*, my involvement in *Big Brothers* would give me the most satisfaction.

I was assigned to be a Big Brother to Tommy Porta, a little nine-year-old, who had no male members in his family to identify with. Tommy, a well-mannered little boy lived with his mother, an older sister and his grandmother. Saturdays was our day, and we spent it going to major league foot ball and base ball games, miniature and par three golf, and the State Fair.

"I want a bicycle, Mr. Braucht," he said one day. I could have easily bought it for him, but I wanted to teach him the responsibility of money, and I knew he would appreciate the bike more if he had to earn the money himself.

"Then how about earning the money for the bike," I told him.

"But I don't know how to do that," he said, looking very disappointed. "And I don't think I can earn one hundred dollars."

"I'll show you how," I said, thinking of ways that he could make the money. "First, how about collecting pop bottles? You can redeem them for money."

Tommy was all smiles.

We drove around parks, fields and the State Fair grounds, and found quite a few redeemable bottles. This was a start. With the money he got from the bottles, I suggested he buy candy from a local wholesale dealer and sell it door to door.

This worked out so well, I suggested he get some of his friends to work for him. On our next venture, we bought one-hundred dozen doughnuts at a local bakery for fifty cents a dozen, and sold door to door for a dollar a dozen. It didn't take a rocket scientist for Tommy to realize he was doubling his money with each sale. He paid his 'hired' help ten cents a box and gave a dollar bonus to whoever sold the most doughnuts.

This was a very successful venture and I believe Tommy learned a valuable lesson, for within a few weeks, he earned

A LIFETIME WORTH REMEMBERING

enough money to buy the bike of his dreams.
 Tommy and I had many adventures together. We entered one contest as a team that was sponsored by Big Brothers. We followed a list of instructions that took us from checkpoint to check point and were the first team to accomplish the assignment according to the exact instructions.
 We each received a plaque and a statue for our efforts.
 Tommy not only graduated from Dixie Holland's High School second in his class, but also was awarded an all expense paid scholarship to Cornell University.

When Tommy turned eighteen, he was out of the Big Brother program, but we have remained friends ever since.
 I am reminded of that young man whenever I look at the Big Brothers award I received for staying with a boy the longest. It was a statue of a man and a boy with the inscription, "For Devotion To The Betterment Of A Young Boy," and my name engraved on the base.
 Tommy made everyone proud when he graduated from Cornell with a degree in engineering. He went to work with NOVA,(National Oceanic and Atmospheric Administration) surveying the shoreline and ocean depths in Alaska.
 Recently I received a letter from Tommy in which he reminisced about our relationship:
 When I was at sea on the NOVA ship, he wrote, *I asked you to send me a tape you made from your Bible Library because I like them better than the other scholar's tapes. You said, 'The other tapes were better', but you sent me your tapes anyway. Mrs. Braucht told you the reason why. It was because I wanted to hear the sound of your voice.*

JOHN BRAUCHT

I am thankful that you taught me the basics of sales and investments. I will never forget the joy of accomplishment I got when I earned enough money to buy my first bike.

Remember when we won the road rally? I was the driver and you were the navigator. The course was based on time, speed and distance. There were times when I thought we were going to lose, but with your navigating we won.

You were always a good friend to me. You were never late for our meetings on Saturdays. You said people learned to rely on you if you did what you said you were going to do.

My friends said their fathers didn't spend as much time with them as you did with me. You took me everywhere, to the beach, bowling, the state fair and Disney World, just to name a few. And I liked helping you work in your garden.

You made me feel good about myself. I remember when we'd meet friends of yours, and you'd tell them how smart I was, or say something good about me.

You taught me never to be discouraged and encouraged me to focus on my good traits.

I don't know what I would have been without my relationship with you. You have been a model for how a good man should behave.

Thank you for being such a good friend to me.
Love, Tom.

"PAN AM FLIGHT 103, VICTIM OF A TERRORIST BOMBING, CRASHES IN LOCKERBIE, SCOTLAND"

Chapter Thirty-Nine
1988

When we visited my parents in 1988, it was obvious that my mother's memory was failing. I asked them to move in with us. At first Dad refused, but I kept after him. Eventually, I wore him down because he called one night, and said, "Come and get us."

I flew out of McDill to Barksdale Air Base the next day. Dad met me at the airport, and the first thing we did was to see an attorney. Dad had him draw up papers that gave me power-of-attorney to dispose of Dad's property.

After I sold his car and house, we hired a moving company to pack and ship their personal possessions and antiques to our house in St. Petersburg.

We decided to fly back to Florida. Mom, who would never fly, gave us no resistance and boarded the plane without incident. When we were airborne and above the clouds, she smiled and said, "This is so wonderful. It must be what

JOHN BRAUCHT

Heaven is like."

They moved in with us on July 12th, which was on Mom's 88th birthday. By now, we had my parents and Lue's mother, Kay, living with us. Lue needed a room to enjoy her growing button hobby and sewing, so we added another room to the house.

I was thankful that I was healthy and active, because the nursing, cooking, laundry, cleaning, and the yard work became my responsibility.

Dad was able to help a little in the yard, but eventually it became too much and I hired a full-time yardman.

Mom had difficulty falling sleep and liked me to sing to her, especially the song, "Count Your Many Blessings".

Mom's health was good, but after a few months her memory began to fail.

"John, where is that guy in the red shirt?" she asked me one day.

"What guy?" I said, wondering whom she was talking about.

"The guy who gave me a potato."

"That was me, Mom. Remember, I'm your son ,John," I said. "But I've got on a white shirt now."

"No, it's not you," she insisted. "He gave me a potato and I want another one."

Mom became so forgetful that she could not remember which room was hers. I made a plaque with her name, and hung it across her door so she could find her room.

It was in the fall of 1988, when my mother fell and broke her hip. By now, she was very fragile and her health was declining rapidly. She passed away quietly in the hospital on

A LIFETIME WORTH REMEMBERING

September 14, at the age of 92.

Dad mourned deeply for her. We were grateful that he was with us during this stressful time. Always a strong and active man, his life long habit of getting up at four in the morning, taking long walks and exercising helped keep his mind and body healthy.

But Dad would pass away on August 19, 1993; two months shy of his 99th birthday.

In 1990, I was diagnosed with cancer. After a year's successful treatment of *Chemotherapy* and *Lavamasol*, I was presented a clean bill of health. I considered myself fortunate that I did not experience nausea or lose my hair.

The doctor was amazed at my rapid recovery and suggested that I tell my story to people who were going through the same treatment.

I joined a Cancer Support Group, and told them what I had been through, and to what I attributed my cure.

"Keep busy, help others and pray a lot," I said. "That's the most powerful medicine you can take."

"And even singing helps," a young boy added.

"You're right, young man," I said. "Worry and stress are killers. The Bible tells us not to let anything worry you.

"If you remember what God says and have a positive attitude, it will help you through this crisis."

Lue suffered from *sciatica* and there were times that the pain grew so bad, she'd cry, "I want to die!"

I'd call 911 and she'd be rushed to the hospital. Since there was no cure, they could only give her shots to deaden the pain.

This gave her only a temporary relief, and before long the pain was back again.

"What can we do?" I asked Doctor Nowakowski. "Nothing seems to work."

He thought for a moment. "Let's give this a try. I'll call in a prescription for a muscle relaxer and," he said turning to Lue, "I want you take it with two Tylenol."

Doctor Nowakowski's advice worked and the pain subsided, but only temporarily. The sciatica comes back every now and then, but Lue is not one to complain and her hobbies keep her busy.

A LIFETIME WORTH REMEMBERING

"THE NEW MILLINIUM"

Chapter Forty
2000

When I returned to the United States from England in 1943 to the present day, our Bible work has grown. It now reaches people around the world. Our goal is to furnish learning material that stresses the need for knowledge, the love of God and help for anyone who needs help.

Although my request to God when I was thirteen to let me be like Paul and preach the Gospel went unanswered, He must have given me a different mission to take. I have been teaching the Bible ever since.

In accomplishing this mission, we put God first. He has blessed me to the point where He never leaves my mind.

The verse that explains how this is done reads:

For the love of Christ is constraining us, judging this, which, if one died for the sake of all, consequently all died. And He died for the sake of all that those who are living should by no means still be living to themselves, but to the

JOHN BRAUCHT

One dying and being roused for their sakes.

We gave all the materials away free until 1970 and returned any donations that we received. In 1980, we decided to incorporate and become a non-profit organization.

In 1974, after so many students insisted on donating to our non-profit corporation, we began to accept the donations for several reasons. First, people wanted to claim the donations as deductions on their income tax and second, they felt guilty accepting the material at our expense.

Lue and I continued to donate forty percent of our personal income to provide books to anyone who could not afford a donation to the business. About ten years ago, we took seventy-nine volumes of books that contain the writings of Greek students as far back as 1909. As of this date, we have a total of ninety volumes.

Sandy, Lue and I proof read each of the volumes carefully, and have transferred them to CD-ROM's. Our work is never done because a new volume is published every year. We have had volunteers proof read the books from California to New Jersey.

Our intent is not to tell people what to think, but to furnish them the materials they need to study.

Sandy Adkins, the daughter of one of the teachers of the Greek text, offered to help us with the business in 1990.

"I don't expect any pay," she said.

"That's very unselfish of you," Lue told her.

We had never paid anyone working for the corporation until 1999 when the board of directors voted to pay

A LIFETIME WORTH REMEMBERING

Sandy a salary.

We realized what a great help she was and promoted her to office manager. We were also getting on in age, and wanted the business to continue in the event that we were no longer able to do so.

"I need you to understand," I told her one day, "that Lue and I want you to manage the corporation in the event that we can't. Is this something that you would agree to?"

"Yes, I'd be happy to take it over for you," she said with a smile. "But I don't think we have to worry about that for quite a few years yet."

Sandy took over as housekeeper, as well as office manager when I was operated on for colon cancer, later in the year. Since she was so involved in the business, and considered one of the family, she brought her little daughter to work with her.

Gene has blessed us with two beautiful granddaughters, two grandsons, and two great grandsons and three great granddaughters.

Ricky, our youngest, has lived a very unselfish life. From the time he was a young man, he contributed food to the needy. He also volunteered to work in a rehabilitation shelter for addicts.

Ricky participated in blind golfer training. At first he and his blind partner were trained separately, and later they were trained together as a team.

Ricky placed his partner in position next to the tee and described the layout of the course. After the blind man selected the correct club, he would make his swing. They completed the course, with low scores; a remarkable feat made possible by having complete confidence in each other's ability.

In addition to the many accomplishments made by Ricky, he also won state boxing championship in his class when he belonged to the Police Athletic Society.

People have asked me through the years why my birth parents abandoned my brothers and me and did I ever find them.

As far as I have been able to find out, my father was a school superintendent who developed tuberculosis when we were in the orphanage and died shortly afterwards. My mother was never heard from again, and it was assumed that she also died.

From time to time, my brothers and I tried to find out more information, but the trails always ended up cold. We were so young when they abandoned us, that it's difficult to remember them at all.

I was fortunate to find parents who were parents in every sense of the word and I could not have loved them any more if they were my biological parents.

I imagine I must have longed for my Papa and Mama and my brothers, but time has dimmed the sadness of those days and, instead, I have chosen to remember the pleasant memories.

In retrospect, I have been blessed with a loving wife. We've had over sixty wonderful and exciting years together. I am as much in love with Lue today as I was the day I first saw her sweet smile…if not more. She is my best friend, and the

A LIFETIME WORTH REMEMBERING

most precious thing in my life.

Lue and I are looking forward to many more years of happiness.

JOHN BRAUCHT

A LIFETIME WORTH REMEMBERING

EPILOGUE

Early in March of the year 2000, Lue and I received a most touching letter from Pastor Orville Griffin, the young man, who became the Pastor of the East Dayton Baptist Church in Dayton.

It reads as follows:

Dear John and Lue,

This material, written by us is for use in your book on your life.

Ten adults and four children met for the purpose of organizing a Baptist Mission in Lawton School, Linden Avenue, Dayton, Ohio on February 28, 1954.

These believers, with a strong conviction that a Southern Baptist Church was needed on the eastside of Dayton, committed themselves to share the Gospel with this section of the city. Another important consideration of this committed group of believers was a witness and ministry to military families living in 'Page Manor' (military housing near Wright Patterson AFB).

For seventeen months, meeting together as East Dayton Baptist Chapel, the believers worshiped, witnessed and added members.They were sponsored by the Westwood Baptist Church on Westwood Avenue in Dayton. At that time, Westwood was the largest Southern Baptist Church not only in the city but also in the state of Ohio.

In the meantime, one of the first priorities was to call a pastor. In October of 1954, I received a telephone call from the Pulpit Committee that would change the direction of my

JOHN BRAUCHT

life for the next 45 years. I did accept the invitation to be the pastor of this new mission of thirty-three people. I served as pastor for a little over twelve years, and later in Ohio Convention as Missionary Church Leader and Executive Director of State Convention of Baptists in Ohio.

The 'Chapel' was organized July 31, 1955 with one-hundred-nine charter members. Among them were four members of the John Braucht family.

As pastor in November of 1954—I worked with families —the original ones beginning East Dayton Chapel (Mission) plus others, John, Luella and sons, Eugene and Ricky. They became pillars of strength and dedication in the early life of the mission, which became East Dayton Baptist Church, 1380 Spaulding Road, Dayton, Ohio.

John was elected to serve as Chairman of the first Steering Committee. This committee would function in place of a board of Deacons, as the Mission was not constituted for seventeen months into a church. This committee served as an Advisory Committee for the young mission. They encouraged and supported their young pastor (almost twenty-three years old).

Many important decisions were made that related to the work and ministry of the Mission'. It did survive and had the impact in the community that the five families had envisioned.

As pastor, I was grateful for this committee and their support, advice and leadership they gave me and the East Dayton Mission.

It was so important and vital to have a man of John Braucht's maturity, wisdom, vision and willingness to serve

A LIFETIME WORTH REMEMBERING

as chairman of this committee during important months in the life of this young mission.

The congregation voted to elect their first deacons, December 1955 after organizing into a church July 31, 1955. John Braucht was one of five men elected to this important position of service and leadership. As he had given to the Steering Committee, John brought a strong spiritual devotion and commitment to the ministry and service as a deacon. He exemplified the true meaning of the word 'Deacon', as he served faithful in the ministry and work of the church. He helped me, as pastor, minister to the spiritual needs of the people.

The church experienced rapid growth in membership and organization. There was the ever-growing need to have our own place of worship and suitable space for Sunday school and other religious educational activities.

The Lawton School had served us well as a rented meeting place. We were grateful for the use of a school because we were able to rent adequate space as we grew in number. But now, the Vision and Prayers were for us to own and build our church building.

These raised two important questions: (1) Where would we build and (2) How to finance the project site and finance the construction?

A committee was appointed to search out a building site. John Braucht was called upon to serve as chairman. The committee under John's leadership recommended the purchasing of three acres of land for the sum of eighty-five hundred dollars. This was 1955!

In today's economy (year 2000) that does not seem to be

JOHN BRAUCHT

a lot of money for three choice acres of land. For the young church (young families), it seemed almost impossible to raise the amount of money in a short period. At that time, banks were reluctant to loan money to small churches (especially Southern Baptists in the North). This group of believers didn't give up so easily.

Under John's leadership, the committee came up with a plan and it worked! He and the other four men (with Lue and other wives in agreement) (I might add) would make personal notes for the money, while some applied their personal insurance policies as collateral. So, on May 23, 1955, the three acres were purchased in the name of the church with a loan from Winters National Bank, Dayton—secured by the personal notes of the committee.

During the next few months, through the faithful giving of the church families, the loan and notes were paid in full. This was a tremendous testimony to the committee and members of the church.

We owned the property but how would we raise and secure enough funds to build the first phase of the new church?

The idea of selling interest bearing bonds was suggested. The church voted to enter the Broadway Bond Program of Church Finance located in Houston, Texas. These bonds were sold to members and friends of the church and if successful, would provide monies for the construction to begin.

To have a successful Bond Selling Campaign, the church needed a very strong committee, led by a confidant, honest and efficient chairman. Once again, the church turned to John Braucht to serve as Chairman of Bond Sales.

Through John's persistent effort and leadership, along

A LIFETIME WORTH REMEMBERING

with William G. Massie, Treasurer, the church sold enough Broadway Bonds to begin construction of the proposed building.

On February 20, 1957— three years after the beginning —a remarkable accomplishment had taken place. 'To God Be The Glory'!

The church realized prayer, vision and dreams were coming true. The first 'Service' at 1380 Spaulding Road, was conducted on September 1, 1957 with three hundred forty-two present in Sunday school. Four-hundred five were in Sunday school the next Sunday morning. We were growing weekly!

Lue was faithful as pianist, vocalist, teacher, Women's Missionary Society worker, cook for many fellowships as well as mother to Gene and Ricky and working with John.

What an accomplishment the church had made in the span of three and one half years. 'To God Be The Glory' and 'Without Him' it would have been impossible. God also uses people to accomplish 'His' great work and 'He' certainly used many gifted and dedicated people in the East Dayton Church.

One of these Christian families were the Brauchts! Only eternity will know what contributions this family made to the work of East Dayton Baptist Church.

John was a wise and mature man of 'the faith' during these years. He was an encourager to me and others. I did seek his counsel from time to time and always found him to be helpful. I'm convinced it was dedicated people like John Braucht that entered my life early in my ministry along with God's Help that enabled me to become an effective pastor,

JOHN BRAUCHT

missionary and church leader. Thank you, John for your long and productive Christian life example.

And the words of our Lord to the faithful servant in Matthew's Gospel (Math. 25.21) can be said of the good and faithful servant John Braucht, 'Well done, thou good and faithful servant. Thou has been faithful over a few things. I will make thee ruler over many things. Enter thou into the Joy of the Lord'.

*Your Christian friends,
Lois & Dr. Orville Griffin*

John and "Dovy" on runningboard of car, circa 1926

John in Boy Scout uniform with puppy

John as teenager with chickens

John in the farm cornfield

John as Cadet

Mrs. Brazil with human skulls in Portobelo

Native girl and baby on one of the Sand Blast Islands

First Date, John and Lue Braucht—1938

John and his mother, Georgia Marie Braucht, circa 1943

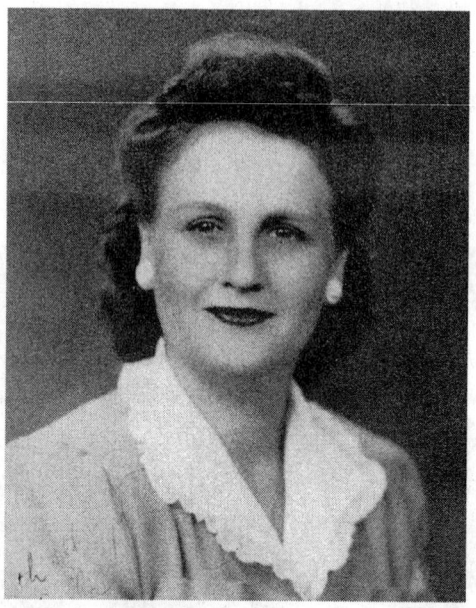

Lue Braucht

Gene Braucht

Ricky Braucht

JWB Publishing Order Blank
For Additional Copies of
A Lifetime Worth Remembering
~ From Orphan to Hero

- Phone Orders Call: (727) 347-2051
- Postal Orders: JWB Publishing
  6201 29th Avenue North
  St. Petersburg, Florida 33710

Please send ___(print number)___ books (at $12.95 ea.). I understand that I may return any books for a full refund.

Sales Tax: None. (Non-profit organization)
Shipping: $3.00 for the first book and $2.00 for each additional book.
Payment: (Please make checks payable to JWB Publishing.)

☐ Mail Order   ☐ Check

E-mail: jbrauch1@tampabay.rr.com

Also Available:
Various Bibles, Concordants, Tapes and Books of Inspiration
(We will research rare books for you.)

Name:_____
Address:_____
City:_____State:_____Zip:_____
Date:_____Telephone: (   ) _____-_____

☐ Please put me on the mailing list.

(Clip and Send)

JWB Publishing Order Blank
For Additional Copies of
A Lifetime Worth Remembering
~ From Orphan to Hero

📞   Phone Orders Call: (727) 347-2051

✉   Postal Orders: JWB Publishing
                          6201 29th Avenue North
                          St. Petersburg, Florida 33710

Please send ___(print number)___ books (at $12.95 ea.). I understand that I may return any books for a full refund.

Sales Tax: None. (Non-profit organization)
Shipping: $3.00 for the first book and $2.00 for each additional book.
Payment: (Please make checks payable to JWB Publishing.)

☐ Mail Order   ☐ Check
         E-mail: jbrauch1@tampabay.rr.com

Also Available:
Various Bibles, Concordants, Tapes and Books of Inspiration
(We will research rare books for you.)

Name:_____
Address:_____
City:_____State:_____Zip:_____
Date:_____Telephone: (____)_____-_____

☐ Please put me on the mailing list.

✂ (Clip and Send)